D0988819

To

With wishes of peace.

/ /

DIVALDO FRANCO
BY THE SPIRIT
VICTOR HUGO

ILL-FATED DIAMONDS

Authorized edition by Centro Espírita Caminho da Redenção.
Salvador (BA) – Brazil

Miami
1st ed. 2020

ISBN 978-1-947179-91-2

Original title in Portuguese:
Os diamantes fatídicos
(Brazil, 2018)

Translated by: Darrel Kimble / Marcia Saiz / Andreia Marshall Netto

Cover design by: Claudio Urpia

Layout by: Rones Lima – instagram.com/bookebooks_designer

Edition of
LEAL PUBLISHER
8425 Biscayne Boulevard, Ste. 104
Miami, FL 33138
www.lealpublisher.com
Phone: (305) 206-6447

Authorized edition by Centro Espírita Caminho da Redenção – Salvador (BA) – Brazil

INTERNATIONAL DATA FOR CATALOGING IN PUBLICATION (ICP)

F895   FRANCO, Divaldo.

     Ill-fated diamonds / By the Spirit Victor Hugo [psychographed by] Divaldo Pereira Franco ; translated by Darrel Kimble/Marcia Saiz/Andreia Marshall Netto – Miami (FL), USA : Leal Publisher, 2020.

     188 p.; 21cm

     Original title: *Os diamantes fatídicos*

     ISBN: 978-1-947179-91-2

     1. Spiritism 2. Psychography. I Franco, Divaldo Pereira, 1927 – II. Title.

CDD 133.9

CONTENTS

ILL-FATED DIAMONDS

Unbridled human ambition, that beloved daughter of exacerbated selfishness, is responsible for countless calamities of every magnitude weighing on the moral economy of earthly society.

Human beings, having held on to the atavisms of the early stage through which they passed, still cling to the petty interests of supremacy and predominance in relation to everything and everyone. Their minds are set on deceitful temporal triumphs, as if life were only meant for enjoying the passions and the ongoing championship of the lust to which they have surrendered.

Rather than struggling or thinking sensibly, they excel at adopting values that corrupt the sentiments, and even though they revel in their standing within their social group, they live troubled lives because they lack inner harmony due to the fallacy to which they have abandoned themselves.

Since they are preoccupied with accumulating fleeting assets, and are dominated by their servility to sensuality, they treacherously deceive and betray others, hurting the feelings and the dignity of those who they see as obstacles to their sordid goals.

The social group, in which they hold an important position, cynically accepts them in a joyful masquerade that is far from real *because its members are all too familiar with the dark pathways that have led them to their own enviable situation, having engaged in similar intrigues themselves.*

Despite the cordial and diplomatic posturing within the group, there is no wholesome fraternity among its members, nor the trust that would be desirable for there to be ideal, complete harmony.

Caring interaction is almost nonexistent because delving into emotional interests is avoided. Such interests are marked with systematic suspicion since each member wants to occupy the lofty position temporarily occupied by someone else.

Very few individuals at this stage are aware of organic transience. They are under the impression that their happiness will last forever, as if they were exceptional beings specially chosen by the gods of Olympus.

Such a vain notion is misleading, for none can escape the cellular mortar in which they are temporarily encased on their pilgrimage through the earthly archipelago as part of their evolutionary process.

The deceitfulness of matter, which seduces so many, does often disperse during the carnal transit itself; however, it always does so after the heart stops beating, followed by the biological phenomenon of death.

Indestructibility is the condition of the spirit, not of the body that clothes it.

The earthly journey is one of learning, education, the development of inner qualities. It is never one of fulfillment, of flawless happiness, because, in any learning institution, individuals experience only the joy of the opportunity, the blessing they derive from their studies as they faithfully prepare themselves for achieving their purpose, at which time they will be able to evaluate the results of their efforts.

All who look for fulfillment in the organic complex and in the accumulation of fleeting things deceive themselves.

As Jesus Christ emphasized, real treasures are those that thieves cannot steal, nor moths devour, nor rust corrupt.

Thus such treasures entail the gifts of the spirit, moral values, the inalienable resources of the soul.

* * *

Down through the ages, rare gems, due to their beauty and consequent monetary value, have exerted a passionate fascination on individuals who have struggled to accumulate them at any cost.

In order to acquire such gems, individuals invest fortunes that could be put to much better use, such as destroying the hunger, disease, ignorance and moral poverty that prevail in the world. Nevertheless, they are transformed into gleaming stones kept in elegant, expensive cases that lie lifeless in strong vaults, to be worn now and then, provoking envy and resentment, while adorning their temporary owners with the sparkle of vanity for a few brief moments.

When they are bearers of purity and perfection – making them even rarer – they are transferred from one person to another, from one generation to the next, some becoming bearers of tragedies, of crimes committed to possess them, rendering them ill-fated for their owners...

Although the drama we chronicle in the following pages has profound causes rooted in previous incarnations, sparkling diamonds, which will incite a number of crimes, play an important role in our true story, a story that has undergone necessary adaptations and modifications to avoid identifying the characters that constitute our novel, some of whom are still incarnate.

Our desire is to show that the power of the Law of Cause and Effect is invincible. It allows none to defraud it, no matter how clever, perverse, or cynical individuals may be, for, wherever they may try to run to, the Law is unappealable as it fulfills the providential mission for which it was programmed.

The effective and sole method for finding real happiness is most assuredly the exercise of right conscience, right activity, and unfaltering moral conduct.

Life charges a price for all the crimes that are committed against its Sovereign Codes.

Therefore, the only alternative left for the human being is to respect it in all its expressions.

Águeda (Piedade, Espinhel, Portugal)
October 20, 2003
Victor Hugo

BOOK ONE

1
THE SPLENDOR
AND DECADENCE
OF A NATION

The 20th century, marked by extraordinary advances in science and technology, can also be seen as the most insolent in regard to the rights of the human being.

The unrest that had gripped humankind since the Industrial Revolution in England and Germany in the 19th century forced the dominant oligarchic traditions to make a hurried revision of concepts and even a few attempts to eliminate castes and privileges, thus leading to immediate changes.

At that time, the flames of *human rights* were being fanned by the French Revolution of 1789 and were being inscribed on the grand pages of justice with unspeakable suffering, breaking the chains of slavery almost completely and acquiring citizenship, thanks to idealist philosophers and zealous politicians, who were no longer bound in the dungeons of wickedness or senseless discrimination.

Russia, subject to the arrogance and autocracy of the Romanovs, externalized its hateful conduct through Tsar

Nicholas II, who boasted about preserving his power with an iron hand, reducing his opponents to pitiable corpses and the proletariat to minimum conditions for survival. The same was the case with the poor, malnourished peasants, whose lives were reaped from the very moment they were born. The Bolshevik Revolution of 1917 promised to offer better days to the workers in the factories and fields, but unfortunately it later degenerated into a new and arbitrary socialist power ruled by the insatiable greed of the politburo.

China, which had suffered under the age-old Manchu rule, slowly sluffed off the heavy, heinous yoke to take a breath of hope as a socialist revolution took over its immense territory, pointing to better possibilities in life for the people. Nevertheless, new rulers assumed command, promoting slave labor, the submission of women, and the murder of newborns, especially females.

Japan, clinging to its heritage as the *Empire of the Rising Sun*, slaughtered its people, who were crushed in the terrible chains of oppression, but it found its arbitrary power dwindling after World War II, submitting to the great power of the United States and opening up to the West.

In all of these countries, women, children, the elderly and the sick were an unwanted burden, from whom their dictators sought release. These individuals' condition was actually that of being *free-slaves,* in that, although they were part of society, they did not enjoy all the same privileges, including freedom of movement. Women, for example, were inferior and looked down on, living solely to serve men.

In light of this dire Eurasian situation, the United States opened its ports to immigration in order to meet the needs of its industrial development. Each and every day, it welcomed foreigners from all over the world: Jews being persecuted in Russia, Italians looking for new opportunities, Irish suffering from endless torment in their homeland, and many other peoples seeking refuge and an opportunity for a richer life...

The British Empire, in its Victorian grandeur, had become the largest in the world, stretching to practically every continent. Its excessive pride, with which it despised everyone who was not British, submitted people to exasperating servility.

India, for example, was one such victim. With 250 million inhabitants still divided into separatist castes, it was ruled by only 5,000 British, who subjected its population to the most shameful humiliations...

In their colonialist madness, France, Belgium, Portugal and Spain did not escape the perverse fury of subjugating peoples who were culturally, economically and politically weak, after having defeated them in tragic wars.

All things considered, such was the dominant socio-culture situation in the most diverse nations, with greater or lesser predominance of hatred and savagery, disguised as civility and ethical behavior, sustaining detestable colonialism in the countries that had been conquered militarily. Everywhere, the poor, the peasantry, the proletariat, the unemployed were regarded as subhuman, rabble that embarrassed the domineering society, despite being at its service in most cases. Robbed by absurd taxes needed to fund the gilded idleness of landowners and their purposes, they were reduced to the miserable condition of being the trash of society – nowadays called the "socially excluded."

New territorial conquests finally declined in importance because it was necessary to exploit the countries that had already been subjugated.

South Africa, with its almost inexhaustible, untapped deposits of diamonds, gold and silver, and later of uranium, also became victim of the British Lion, which seized it from the arbitrary Dutch governance, in whose clutches its autochthons had suffered, losing any and all rights in their homeland, including that of free movement.

Europeans had known about South Africa since 1488, when the Cape of Good Hope – formerly called Cape of Storms by the Portuguese navigator Bartolomeu Dias – was discovered, but it was only around 1652 that the first European settlements were started by the Dutch East India Company. They remained in control until about 1795, when they were defeated by a British force that took over the colony...

The heinous apartheid[1] was the best solution the dominators could find to use against the inhabitants of the land that had been stolen from them after the truculent and wicked Boer[2] War passed permanent control to the British crown, making the former owners regarded as reprobates. The more the slave-holders' presumptuousness increased, the more overbearing and haughtier they became. They ended up creating veritable segregation camps, into which the suffering country's inhabitants were herded like human cattle after 6:00 p.m., and allowed to leave only the next morning.

Subsequently, because the aberration exceeded the limits bearable by the other nations of the earth, "countries" were created within the South African territory for the various black ethnicities, segregating them more and more: Bophuthatswana (its capital Mmabatho), Transkei (capital Umtata [Mthatha]), where Nelson Mandela was born, Venda

---

1   Apartheid - Separate development (spirit author's note)
2   Boers – Name given to the Dutch (publisher's note)

(capital Thohoyandou), and Ciskei (capital Bhisho) were some of those established by the new owners in their cruelty, keeping their fellow human beings subjected with no respect whatsoever, reduced to almost nothing...

Only after excruciating struggles and the sacrifices of thousands of lives, who fell helpless into the evil hands of the rulers, did those who had been subjected finally acquire independence and citizenship from 1977 to 1981. However, they were incapable of self-governance after so many years of suffering and slavery.

Weighing favorably on its spiritual economy, shortly before its liberation South Africa opened its borders to Portuguese colonialists who had been living in, or had been born in, Angola, when, after the famous 25 April 1974[3], its native inhabitants unleashed a no-less-cruel persecution on their former masters.

Receiving tens of thousands of fugitives who were collected into veritable internment camps – albeit with dignity and work – South Africa enabled many of them to recover their moral worth by honoring themselves with the sweat of their own brows, working for the progress of the new, generous country that had stretched out its protective arms to them...

No one, however, can hinder the moral evolution of society. Consequently, liberating movements have emerged, responsible for modifying the current harmful social structure of the planet, although many people remain subjected and scorned by the indifference of the great powers.

---

3   Reference to the Carnation Revolution in Portugal. "In the wake of the revolution, a rapid and hasty programme of decolonisation was pushed through; over the next few years, Guinea-Bissau, Mozambique, Cape Verde Islands, Sao Tome and Principe and Angola were all granted independence" (http://www. onthisdeity.com/25th-april-1974---the-carnation-revolution/) – Tr.

After exhaustive struggles, the movement for female suffrage in the United States gave women their right as citizens and recognition for the worth they possess and must exercise in society.

The yoke of oppression began to be shaken from the shoulders of its victims, opening the way for more-audacious flights in the future.

The revolution of thought, fomented by idealists, materialized in charismatic and unique leaders, who rose to throw off the arbitrary and inhuman yoke that the powerful nations exerted over those whose rights had been mercilessly seized by civilized assailants.

The emergence of the United Nations materialized cultured aspirations for the benefit of a more harmonious humanity. It focused on healthy, political social justice programs, which time will make a reality after bloodthirsty dictators and usurpers have yielded their arbitrary place to dignified and balanced individuals.

The first big step, however, had been taken, and slowly the shadows of perversity and domination would give way to the light of a New Era, which will reach its peak in the not too distant future.

Of course, inequalities and crimes that shock modern day minds still exist, but this demonstrates the primitiveness that still thrives in human beings alongside their incalculable conquests of knowledge in all areas.

But if we examine those still-recent days of shocking barbarism, we can get an idea of how they will be seen in the not too distant future by those who will come after us.

The moral processes of evolution are undeniably slower than those of a technological and scientific nature, whose reflections are perceived by the external being, whereas those of an emotional, internal nature are not always immediately detected, although they represent the true achievements of the human being.

Unfortunately, men and women still bear the ancestral legacies of arbitrary actions and abuses committed against their neighbor, and they have not been able to preserve the achievements of their forbearers, who opened pathways for democracy, the right to come and go from place to place, and the respect for ethical and cultural values.

Consequently, as soon as they are given a prominent position in society, they release the passions that yet remain in their inner world and they try to repeat the injurious exploits of the not too distant past.

The recent, shameful examples of Adolf Hitler, Mussolini, Hirohito, the Khmer Rouge and many other such murderers of their people and of humanity demonstrate that there is not yet enough psychological, psychical and moral maturity to hinder such vile tendencies, supported, no doubt, by millions of sympathizers and supporters of their barbarities, keeping them in power, though temporarily. Death interrupted the existence of some of these assassins of humanity; the uprising of exhausted victims gripped in their claws overthrew many from their thrones of lies; and the infirmities that strike everyone reduced the rest to lamentable conditions – the world was finally released from their heinous presences.

Nevertheless, in an attempt to obstruct or impede the irrefragable advance of progress, such criminals frequently reappear in disguise to bribe consciences, consume hopes, and destroy the ideals of life of many who struggle. But of course they will fail.

At the same time, high-order spirits don the carnal apparel and immerse themselves in the darkness of the earth in order to ignite stars of courage and freedom, justice and fraternity, while preserving human rights – still violated, but never destroyed – in preparation for the happy days of the future.

Not all of them have been able to bear the pressure of their peers, however. Often, as happened with Lenin, Marx and Trotsky, their philosophical ideals morphed into bloody struggles, necessary at the time, and they became new murderers of the defenseless masses, under the iron glove of the delusion that gripped some of them in vengeance and the ravings of madness.

But despite such dreadful failures, Mohandas Karamchand Gandhi, Martin Luther King Jr., Nelson Rolihlahla Mandela and countless anonymous heroes were able to hold on to the values that inspired them and never let themselves descend into the criminality they had come to fight, the slavery they had come to abolish, or the subjection whose bonds they had come to break. They continue to be models of how new generations can establish the liberating movement of consciences and lives on the earth.

Russia, which had brought millions out of misery to make them dignified and happy citizens, endured atheistic, perverse Communism under Stalin and his successors, who enslaved the country's inhabitants and sent astonishing, countless numbers to Siberia, asylums and death because they were seen as political enemies, thus repeating the shameful tragedy of the insensitive Romanovs.

China, under Mao Zedong, opposed culture and freedom, and stoked a fire of intolerance and hatred directed at the past, burning its books and trying to destroy its multi-millennial traditions, which, alongside gains in contemporary art, are slowly being recovered, in spite of the arrogance that governs the country.

Japan, subjected to U.S. power, woke up to modernity and revolutionized its industry through advanced technology, opening itself up to international trade and exchange, enabling other Asian nations to follow behind.

Vile colonialism left its marks of horror all over Africa, various Asiatic countries, and Latin America, all enduring the worst persecutions, despite yearning for independence. And its aftermath continues to ruin lives. With the perversity of exploitation, the dominators of these lands and lives did not permit national idealists to develop their dreams of happiness, but murdered, persecuted and exiled them instead. And when social progress did bring freedom, there were neither thinkers nor politicians capable of developing dormant values in order to move with confidence and skill amid international affairs. Hence they became easy prey to the economic interests of other peoples, plunging into civil wars of uncommon cruelty, which still continue to rend the flesh from their souls.

Nearly the whole continent of Africa suffers from this incomparable scourge, with the savage, destructive persecutions of one ethnicity against another, as is the case with the Tutsi and Hutu, the Nigerians, the Congolese and many others...

Moreover, supported by the interests of former rulers or of new dominators, beastly individuals are put in power, satiating themselves on their subjects' ignorance in order to torment them even more, feasting on truculent spectacles of anthropophagy, as occurred with Idi Amin Dada – former dictator of Uganda, who, in his eight years, massacred about

300 thousand people – and Jean-Bédel Bokassa – who crowned himself emperor of the Central African Republic and ruled for thirteen years. Divested of their power, such individuals sought political asylum in tax havens or nations that should have stood up for the human rights they proclaimed, as was the case with France, which gave many of them refuge in order to benefit from their assets bathed in the blood and tears of the despoiled. Bokassa, deposed in 1969, could not escape his biological fate and discarnated in 1996.

Tragic tribal struggles have corrupted nearly every country in black Africa, especially struggles between the previously mentioned Tutsi and Hutu tribes, generating what became known as Africa's First World War.

Mozambique and Angola dreamed of freedom and then achieved it without bloodshed, but then became drunk on the sordid passions of political parties that were more interested in exhausting their countries' riches, plunging them into internal wars of unpredictable consequences.

Even today, Angola is considered the country with the highest number of landmines, harvesting the lives of its inhabitants, who exist under a fraudulent peace and the subaltern interests of foreign rulers.

Nationalist uprisings continue to erupt all over the world, inviting the ambitious to ponder, at times too late, having imposed themselves on those who have the right to freedom in their homeland, in spite of having been beaten down by infamous wars or by the wiles of their hated rulers.

Among these rulers are those of the most deplorable religious, prejudicial and absurd beliefs, who are always grieving humankind, astonished by the brutality of the human heart, as occurred in the former Yugoslavia, Lebanon, Libya,

Chechnya, Palestine, and in Iraq against the Kurds, who were practically wiped out with bacteriological and chemical bombs, although the country is now under U.S. oversight; in Haiti, under the dynasty initiated by its insensible head, the physician Papa Doc, and then his son Baby Doc...

Primitivism, which still predominates in human nature, is responsible for the arbitrariness and senselessness still being committed, often under the guise of human rights...

South Africa, however, ill-prepared for self-government after breaking free of racial segregation and white domination, currently suffers the no-less-unfortunate consequences of hatred between the different ethnicities and that of all those that are united against their old oppressor.

From towns and neighborhoods like Soweto – famous for the deaths of their heroes – which have remained fixed in the memory of the past, the unemployed and criminals flock to the large cities, making them open battlefields of cruelty. Their police forces are unprepared and unable to offer the least amount of safety to their citizens, who work and pay taxes to have freedom of movement, liberty, and technological and cultural development.

The monumental figure of Nelson Mandela remains a symbol of someone who suffered oppression for almost thirty years in solitary jails, without his voice being silenced. As the first black president of his beloved country, he was unable to advance it, because the torturous effects of so many years of slavery could not be eliminated in such a brief period of balanced leadership. Although the country is vigilant and continues to dream, it obviously suffers from national decadence for lack of capable politicians, with some interested in revenge, and others in illicit enrichment, despite the honesty of many and the dignity of a large number of nationalist servants of the legitimate ideals of society...

All of its riches in disarray and its currency in constant devaluation are urgent concerns in the minds and hearts of its inhabitants, who love their homeland, hoping to stave off its painful twilight and a new type of slavery that has been imposed by the wicked capitalism of powerful nations through loans with extortive interest rates, never allowing one to rid oneself of ever-increasing debt, in the illusion that it can be paid off someday...

Even with the suffocation that dominates the glorious country, with the misuse of the wealth derived from immense deposits of gold, diamonds and uranium, after such decline a new dawn will emerge. Its generous soil will welcome its former usurpers – as is already occurring – due to the inalienable demands of reincarnation, in order for them to redeem the terrible crimes they committed in the past, whereas their victims will assume leadership of the nation's destiny, using mercy, compassion and work so that they may dignify themselves and return to the sublime bosom of spiritual freedom.

Such decay also marked the great peoples and their empires in the past, such as the Assyrian, Babylonian, Chaldean, Egyptian, Medo-Persian, Carthaginian, Greek, Macedonian, Roman... and more recently the Union of Soviet Socialist Republics, in whose territory many former enslaved nations and multitudes of victims killed in the Gulag archipelago still weep...

Everything, however, dies to be reborn under other conditions: people, social groups, nations, planets, galaxies, in the endeavor of maintaining universal harmony, which continues to escape us all, backward spirits that we are.

2
AN OPPORTUNITY FOR HAPPY PROGRESS

Manuel Rodríguez, better known as Manolo, was young and a victim of psychotic disorders, which constant doses of alcohol made much worse. A lover of adventure, he was characterized by the extravagances he allowed himself.

He had descended from a group of Spaniards that had emigrated to South Africa in search of better possibilities in life and dreams of fortune, and his father had managed to glean some economic independence by means of a flourishing company he had built in the then prosperous city of V...

The third child of the marriage between Giménez and Santiaga Rodríguez, and the second male, Manolo was brash and personable, although he was not at all physically attractive. Talkative and easy-going, especially when stimulated by a few shots of whiskey, he was ingratiating and able to captivate the eligible young women who attributed to him possession of a fortune that was far from real.

By working with his father, he had accumulated enough financial resources to provide him with a life of pleasure and standing in the Latin community, as the Portuguese and Spaniards in the country were considered.

Those were days of prosperity in South Africa, which had received a large contingent of Portuguese seeking refuge after the liberation of the overseas Lusitanian colonies, maintained ever since the Age of Discovery.

After these *foreigners* had adapted to the locale and had overcome great traumas and suffering, they connected with other immigrants and built their own particular *ghetto,* which provided them with a life full of possibilities.

Tireless workers, they easily assimilated the habits of the new country, despite the cultural and idiomatic difficulties, and managed to develop and promote their own industrial park, which enabled them to maintain a life enriched with hopes, and which, with effort, would make it possible for them to reside in the metropolis in the future.

In preserving their traditions, the Spanish and Portuguese stood out for their affable, open and jovial spirit, winning the hearts of the Afrikaans, who loved the immense Iberian joy of living, as well as its exuberant and delicious cuisine.

The Albuquerque family, in turn, had arrived in the city after a harsh time in the refugee camp, where all experienced many sufferings. But the family had been tenacious enough to recoup assets they had abandoned before Angola's stormy uprising. The need to leave everything behind in order to hold on to their lives had forced them to flee desperately with as little as possible in an old used car, which was unable to make it through the Kalahari Desert in Botswana. They had been saved by volunteers and troops stationed there by the South Africans, who led them, like thousands of others, to refugee camps where they would be housed until they could enjoy the right to work and rebuild a home.

Dr. Henrique Albuquerque was a distinguished man. He had been a magistrate after having left the Catholic priesthood in a beautiful city in the south of Angola, where he enjoyed social, intellectual and economic prestige.

A devout Christian, he had shaped his character by reading and studying the Gospels. They fascinated him and he enriched himself with the philosophical and moral postulates proposed by the Incomparable Man of Nazareth. His wife, Evangelina, had come from a previous marriage that had ended in a stormy divorce, in which she received custody of her two children: Eneida and Júlio.

Eneida was a slender, blond twenty-year-old. Sensitive and well-educated, she was a dreamer and knew the house work, which she had learned from her mother, a woman dedicated to her family and a strong advocate of her children's rights, although marked by minor nervous irritations, some of which were due to obsessive spiritual disorders.

Júlio was introverted and was prone to depression, though he was composed of noble sentiments and an upright character. He had a great capacity for work, which he used to help reconstruct the family's life. Deeply connected to his sister by an age-old affinity that preceded the cradle, he was her veritable guardian angel.

Dr. Albuquerque and Júlio resumed their professional activities in a steel foundry, performing challenging tasks that required unusual and exhausting effort. The machines never stopped and both of them worked the nightshift, after which they always went home exhausted, resting as much as they could during the daylight hours. Even so, the pay was motivation enough for their sacrifice.

Attending the Saturday night social parties at the Latin Club, Eneida and Júlio won over several members of the community, especially Manolo, who, at the first opportunity, approached Eneida and Júlio and had no qualms about communicating his enthusiasm for the young woman. As was natural, she was reserved at first, but the Spaniard's gallantry took effect, and sensing that she was being courted, she could not hide the joy that had invaded her.

Invisible hands were guiding their destinies, a fact that would play a specific role in the building up of their spiritual future.

Manolo was impatient. A few days after their first meeting, he asked to be introduced to Eneida's parents, and was received with distinction and respect. However, unscrupulous and vice-prone, though fascinated by the pursuit of love, he did not completely abandon all his pernicious habits. He still pursued disturbing relationships with sexual partners and continued using alcohol, which would eventually exhaust his physical endurance and fragile moral forces.

Eneida gradually understood her boyfriend's weaknesses and tried to use persuasion to influence him positively to change his behavior, which, in a way, she managed to do temporarily.

While the flame of longing toward his beloved burned within him, the young man sought to temper his attitudes so as to avoid problems with her austere family.

* * *

The country, experiencing reactions against apartheid, was facing problems in the peripheral neighborhoods where the autochthones lived, the true owners of the lands that had been torn from them through shameful, bloody struggles.

A string of attacks in the large cities and ghettos, where the Zulus and other ethnic groups barely survived, led the authorities to decree a curfew after 6:00 p.m., in an attempt to prevent the nationalist reactions of many heroes who were sacrificing themselves in the name of freedom.

When freedom spreads its wings over the oppressed, it imposes such sacrifices on them through grandiose and constant acts of heroism that such acts inspire humanity and end up humbling the enslavers.

The harsher the oppression is, the greater the yearning of its victims for freedom. Thanks to this sentiment, many noble individuals, in their dreams and needs, draw up sublime guidelines for their rights as citizens and human beings.

The so-called "separate development" was not imposed only on the natives, but also on the Asians and Hindus that inhabited the country, and the Mozambicans who worked in the mines... Although they resided in special neighborhoods that were accepted by the white community, they were contemptuously despised and regarded as inferior, devoting themselves to functions that were seen as degrading, but essential to the survival and development of the dominators.

The Iberians were accepted but were not considered worthy of social co-mingling. They were not disturbed by this perverse prejudice, however, because they themselves were not interested in remaining *sine die* as residents of the great African homeland. On their part, they actually detested the Afrikaners as unhygienic, presumptuous and cowardly.

The Afrikaners were bearers of a fundamentalist religious culture, which prohibited the use of alcoholic beverages from Saturday night through Sunday. Nevertheless, on the day before, addicts would acquire the substances they enjoyed, yielding to their dependencies during the period of prohibition. In addition, sidestepping the hypocritical law of abstinence, the wealthy would flee on weekends to Sun City and its fabulous casino. Everything was allowed because the city was exempt from the law, since it was located in the state of Bophuthatswana. The casino was a disgrace to the prevailing poverty of its black population, abandoned almost to its own luck.

South Africa formerly belonged to the British Commonwealth, which ended on or about March 15, 1961, after a referendum replaced the monarchy with a republic. Thus, its white inhabitants lived according to English habits, especially those of a religious nature, although other belief systems and practices were tolerated, such as those of the primitive autochtones (animism) and various expressions of spiritualism, along with the Dutch Reformed Churches, Catholics, Anglicans, Methodists, Jews, and other minorities such as Brahmans, Buddhists and Muslims. There were churches that preserved the ancestral rituals, but practiced activities involving clairvoyance,[4] where good mediums*, in trance or in a state of lucidity, would communicate with discarnates, offering clarifications and narratives, some of which were authentic, whereas others were not, but they were always well-attended events.

Let the truth be expressed: on these occasions, high-order spirits would bring various discarnates to comfort their bereaved relatives and those who were uncertain about the continuance of life after molecular disjunction through the phenomenon of biological death.

---

4   Seeing mediums. *The Mediums' Book*, Allan Kardec CHAPTER XIV, 3rd. Edition, International Spiritist Council, 2009.
* Medium – (from the Latin, *medium*, middle, intermediary). A person who can serve as an intermediary between spirits and incarnates. (Ibid)

God's compassion is infinite. It extends to individuals even when they are not worthily attuned to him, as one would wish.

Thus, discarnate spirits swarm around human beings in an endeavor to demonstrate their survival after physical death by seeking to communicate with loved ones they have left behind and who are filled with longing for them... Whenever the occasion presents itself, they return, offering the comfort of their tenderness and love in a way that upholds those who are fragile and bewildered in light of their death.

Lamentably, however, there are many mediums who benefit financially from their ability. They believe that the time they spend on the ministry of exchange should provide them with a material stipend, since they would be financially compensated if they were employed elsewhere. Well, they should devote themselves to other ways of making money, reserving hours of rest and breaks between tasks to exercise their mediumship so that they may offer it at no charge, in the same way that they have received it from the Supreme Giver.

As long as selfishness is indicative of the conduct of human beings, they will find it difficult to understand the greatness of selflessness toward their neighbor, of self-denial, of unwavering charity... But in the very near future, with their morals renewed for the better, these values will be absorbed naturally by society, as is already the case with those who have discovered a grandiose task of love and dedication in their mediumistic work, in which they reinforce ethical-moral sentiments, with the consequent personal experience.

Without faulting other belief systems and entities, those spiritualistic churches were thus a true refuge for the suffering, who were renewed by the inflow of communications from their discarnate loved ones.

Religious belief is a liniment for afflictions, even when it seems somewhat irrational. Human beings need to believe in something that transcends physical life, something that cannot be immediately decoded. The errors, found in all of them, derive from the pettiness of their clerics, some who are irrational, others, unbalanced, and many, dishonest, etc... However, faithful and devoted believers, attuned to the Higher Powers of the spirit world, always receive answers to their prayers according to their degree of merit.

Were it not for such refuge, despair would assail the masses with dismay, driving them mad, to the worst belligerence and cruelty, for lack of a purpose for their physical lives – as is the case nowadays to some extent.

The Albuquerques were connected with the Catholic Faith, although they did not go to church.

Evangelina experienced continuous obsessive torments because she was a psychophonic[5] medium, and would sometimes go into a spontaneous trance, during which a number of discarnate friends would communicate, offering worthy guidance and urging the family to take up the study of Spiritism, which they knew virtually nothing about. Stubborn and careless, she hesitated to adopt the new Doctrine, although Dr. Albuquerque was sincerely interested in delving into its philosophical and moral postulates, fascinated as he was by their Christian connection. He had been pleasantly surprised by the scientific parameters on which the Doctrine was based, and had immersed himself in studying it.

---

5   Communication by spirits through the voice of a speaking medium. Chapter XXXII, *SPIRITIST GLOSSARY, Allan Kardec The Mediums' Book,* 3rd. Edition, International Spiritist Council, 2009.

The family gathered weekly to pray, read and meditate on Spiritist teachings, especially those found in *The Gospel according to Spiritism* by Allan Kardec. Immediately thereafter, Evangelina would invariably go into a trance, facilitating communications by benevolent benefactors from the Greater World. Among these was a prominent religious emeritus, who had been an anthropologist in Angola and a great researcher of the cultures, habits, languages and behaviors of that country's various ethnic groups, such as the Bantu, Ganguelas, Quanhamas, Mucubais, Bailundos... Nevertheless, the predominant race in the colony was comprised of Hottentots, Kongos and Kaffirs,[6] some in a state of almost complete primitivism...

The spirit, Monsignor Alves da Cunha, always addressed topics of high relevance, which were above Evangelina's level of education, in preparation for timely philosophical, theological and anthropological discussions with Dr. Albuquerque, who was fascinated by these happy opportunities.

From time to time, suffering spirits, disturbed as to what had happened to them, presented themselves just as they were, asking for guidance and help. They were affectionately assisted by the kindly academic. Although unaware of Spiritist doctrinal techniques, he applied psychotherapeutic methods through which the communicators felt renewed. And whenever they returned, their state of affliction had improved significantly.

The family was slowly emerging from the darkness of ignorance, and was moving toward the gratifying light of spiritual knowledge.

---

6   The terms Hottentots and Kaffir are now considered derogatory and have been replaced by the proper terms Khoikhoi and Bantus; however, to keep the integrity of the original text reflecting the terminology of the times, the original terms were maintained. – Tr.

Manolo was presumptuous and ignorant concerning the Spiritist teachings. He was linked more to the ritualistic doctrine he professed, although his faith was not authentic, nor was his moral conduct in line with it. When he became aware of the meetings that took place in his girlfriend's home, he immediately stated that he was opposed to them, as if he could interfere in the conduct of the family, with which he sought identification and commitment. Thinking it was witchcraft, or at least occultism, he did not try to disguise how uncomfortable he was, as if he had the means of discernment to take a religious stand in any debate of such nature.

At his adoptive daughter's suggestion, Dr. Albuquerque invited Manolo to a direct conversation in order to explain to him what the meetings were all about, but faithfully stating that he would never allow anyone to intrude on activities in his own home. He made it clear that Manolo would be very well received unless he tried to interfere in the decisions of that always respectable and deeply Christian family. Warned with severity, with no room for his usual lightheartedness, Manolo seemed to agree, but remained inwardly indignant, believing he had been reproached by his host, which, in fact, he had.

Affective events, however, took place within a harmonious climate, gradually deepening the feelings of affection between the two young people.

Less than five months after their first meeting, Manolo decided to ask for his girlfriend's hand in marriage. A date was set for the wedding, to the delight of both families.

Manolo's parents saw in that decision a chance for tranquility in their home, since the young man often caused domestic problems when he had had too much to drink. As a result of the upcoming marriage, he would have its own home, putting an end to the unpleasant scenes that had become habitual and irrepressible.

The relationship between the Albuquerque and Rodríguez families became friendly and enriching, in spite of their cultural and – why not say it? – educational differences. The members of Eneida's family were more refined. They were more used to having wholesome conversations in cultural circles and being part of a more select society. Their friends, on the other hand, were socially more committed to economic interests and only wanted to exploit the *Blacks,* as they mockingly called those who worked in their industry. They were insensitive and somewhat crass, unable to stand an edifying conversation for very long before steering it toward slander, cruelty, and debauchery.

Dr. Albuquerque foresaw the drama that would develop in the relationship between Eneida and Manolo, but after counseling her, he encouraged her to hold on to her moral and social gifts in order to remain dignified and to preserve the habits of the family in which she had been raised.

The young woman obediently tried to live up to her family's trust in her. Nevertheless, as her fiancé began showering her with caresses and gifts, he also began demonstrating his venal character, becoming jealous, demanding and, at times, downright mean.

Her mother tried to warn her and suggested that she break off the engagement while she still could, but the naive girl replied that, over time and by their living together, she would be able to change her husband.

This is a very common belief among lovers. In their dreams, they believe they can change their partner's deplorable temperaments and liabilities through love and tenderness.

They do not realize that, after the initial feelings of the relationship have passed, partners who are vicious and petty always return to their old, familiar ways. Of course, there are rare exceptions, but in general, such is the case.

The day of the wedding drew near. And as the ceremony was being prepared and the future residence was being organized – it had been built quickly and tastefully – the young Spaniard's impulses increasingly revealed the hazards to which Eneida would be subjected.

In his delirium, he would make accusations against his future mother-in-law, causing malaise, or he would talk rudely about Dr. Albuquerque, demonstrating his emotional instability.

Manolo was a schizoid biotype, and as we have already stated, a victim of negative spiritual incursions into his reprehensible conduct.

Sensing his growing mental disarray, Eneida suggested postponing the wedding. However, she was unable to dissuade him from the desire to "pluck her from that home in which she seemed entombed," as he sometimes expressed himself.

This attitude really worried her, and eventually she confided in her mother that she had been unaware of how imbalanced he actually was.

Concerned, Evangelina suggested cancelling the marriage, since there would be opportunities for other romances. Calling off the marriage would prevent any future occurrence that would prove to be irreversible and unfortunate.

However, after trying to dissuade her fiancé, Eneida gave in to his explanations that he was eager to have her by his side, to build a happy family, regardless of the limitations imposed on her by society and by her family meddling in their relationship.

But the truth was otherwise. Manolo's sentiments were conflicted: he loved Eneida, but did not trust her relationship with her own brother, keeping himself ragingly jealous and highly suspicious. In addition, he had a vague and disturbing impression of some event that he could not identify, one that was dragging him into his beloved's arms but causing him to repudiate her at the same time. As if he had been the victim of some ruse, which he could not pinpoint exactly, he planned to keep her trapped in her golden cage as soon as they were married and she was by his side.

He would smile while pondering such thoughts, donning a sinister mask on a face deformed by some unknown resentment. He would think of dominating her, submitting her to his passions, enslaving her...

In the succession of days, the wedding date finally arrived. The day before, to the surprise of the Albuquerques, Manolo gave his bride-to-be a wedding gift consisting of a diamond necklace and other jewelry, the fruit of his stubborn eagerness to appear wealthier than he really was. He had acquired it with enormous effort, contracting a very heavy debt, which he intended to pay back over the coming months. This detail, however, was unknown to Eneida's family, but she was beside herself with happiness.

According to Manolo's instructions, she was to sport the beautiful necklace, accompanied by a pair of diamond earrings, a bracelet and a ring at the wedding ceremony.

In accordance with their faith, the wedding service was held in a Catholic church and was attended by the cream of the Latin community. Right afterwards, then and there, the civil contract was sealed amid applause and promises of happiness. After the ceremony, there was an elaborate reception at the bride and groom's residence, which had been completed a week before and carefully decorated for this peak moment.

As the guests gathered for the high-quality buffet, the waiters filled their glasses with champagne and whiskey and served them delicious canapés. Then, it was time to cut the wedding cake and toss the bouquet, to be caught by the anxious hands of candidates for future marriages. Amid the enthusiasm and disorder, Eneida and her fiancé changed clothes and fled by car to spend their honeymoon in a luxury hotel, booked beforehand, far from acquaintances.

To cries of happiness and under a delicate shower of rice, the newly-weds headed towards the future.

The festive smiles promised happiness. Manolo had had a little too much to drink, making him overly euphoric. Eneida, however, had almost gotten used to the extravagance and sudden changes in her lover's behavior, but did not realize the danger of his driving a vehicle in that state. After all, she was filled with the dream of conjugal bliss, which everyone yearns for as a supplement to a full life on their evolutionary journey on earth.

3
FIRST GREAT AFFLICTIONS

South African laws, and indeed all such laws worldwide, were very strict, especially those relating to traffic, and in particular as regards operating vehicles with high levels of alcohol in the driver's body.

As the couple headed to Johannesburg, that glorious city surrounded by gold mines displaying their mountains of waste – giving the impression of lunar constructions – resulting from the removal of the precious metal, Manolo was unable to keep the car headed straight down the road. He often swerved into the opposite lane, to the surprise of his frightened wife, while he smiled euphorically, implying that he was doing it for fun. But the reality was quite different. He was actually half drunk and entering into a state of torpor. Shortly before reaching the city, he failed to stop for a red light, catching the attention of a vigilant policeman, who gave chase, realizing that something was wrong. After turning on the siren, he motioned Manolo to pull over, which he did, initiating an unpleasant moment for Eneida, who was unaccustomed to such scenes.

Annoyed and arrogant, Manolo tried to argue with the officer, who ordered him to go with him to the nearest police station, to Eneida's great embarrassment. Manolo was unable to conceal his anger. He had become accustomed to concessions by his family, who had come to fear his bad moods, so he proudly and recklessly confronted the authorities, but was rebuked harshly and warned to remain silent. He was required to be tested for alcohol intake, which was found to be above the legal limit.

In tears, Eneida told the officer that it was a wedding trip, interceding on behalf of her inebriated husband, who was forced to sign off on the fines imposed on him for having run the red light, speeding and disrespecting authority... Moreover, Manolo's car would be impounded at the police station until he recovered; until then, he could not drive.

Thanks to the understanding of the officer, the couple was allowed to call for a rental car to proceed to the luxury hotel, where a special room was reserved solely for newlyweds.

Understandably, the joy-filled emotions from the unusual marriage had disappeared, replaced by nervous fatigue after the incident, which could have been avoided had the young man's morals been different.

Even so, he endeavored to mitigate the unfortunate consequences by treating his beloved consort with kindness and cheerfulness. After a refreshing shower, he promised her he would change his conduct for the better so that theirs would be a happy communion forever.

Unfortunately, on earth, everything that is "forever" is ephemeral, even when it refers to love, which for many entails constant sensations and ungoverned passions that are meant to be satiated. As long as there are reciprocal and pleasant interests in the economy of such relationships, these sentiments last until the moment when new desires accost the individual. Then, there is transference to other levels of enjoyment, involving a thirst for something as new as the former experience was...

Although Manolo was now in a good mood, his unwarranted argument with the policeman and the aggressiveness that he had revealed frightened Eneida and somewhat sullied her illusion of peace.

The wedding night was adorned with earthy charms, with violins during a candlelight dinner in the antechamber of the luxurious room and excellent service by skillful room attendants.

Finding this new reality attractive, Eneida let herself whirl in fascination to the music of fantasy and dreams, as is natural, and then fell joyfully asleep with the help of the good fairy, away from the lingering lethargy that had been imposed on her by the sorcery of the wicked witch.

The next day, the newly-weds wanted to forget about the unpleasant events of the previous day, and went back to the police station to retrieve their car. At Eneida's urging, Manolo apologized to the officer, who kindly received him, realizing that many unhappy acts are imposed on individuals by alcohol. Thus ended well what could have caused real problems.

That afternoon they went shopping, which is usually part of the social menu for many women. But they did not actually need anything; even more, they did not even have time to examine the numerous wedding gifts they had received the day before. However, a great emotional need led them to walk along the city's well-kept streets lined with expensive shops specializing in famous labels.

A sort of negative spell, unknown till now, accompanied the wistful couple.

When the newlyweds went into the jewelry store where Manolo had bought the diamond necklace that Eneida had worn at the wedding, and began discussing the value and beauty of other stones, a gorgeous young model approached them, and without the least bit of modesty, shocked both the saleswoman and Eneida by kissing Manolo on the cheek.

Manolo pushed her away without looking at her, but when he did, he went deathly pale.

The brazen girl smiled mockingly and asked shamelessly:

"Well now, is this the lucky one you exchanged me for? Introduce me. Actually, that won't be necessary. I'll do it myself."

She held out her right hand with a sarcastic look and said:

"I'm his favorite lover girl. I always take care of him on his trips here. He warned me that he was about to get married and said we would have to stop seeing each other. I'm happy I got the chance to run into the two of you." Then, she turned to Eneida and added, "I wish you the best of luck; the same I've enjoyed till now."

Eneida could not move or say one word. She froze, appalled.

Manolo began rebuking the model, and if the manager had not stepped in to calm things down, there would have been a serious incident, besides the one of a moral nature.

The young woman, obviously disturbed and wanting to cause a scene, was skillfully escorted out. The newlyweds were mute, deeply embarrassed.

There are situations where words only make matters worse.

Feeling highly insulted and trembling, Eneida, stood up with the help of the clerk, who offered her a glass of cold water.

Without a word, she and Manolo went back to the car parked out front and he drove them back to the hotel.

A cloud of pain and anguish covered the joys of the day before and reduced expectations of happiness for the future.

Eneida just wanted to go home, to feel the warmth of her family, the comforting kindness of her brother, and the sure guidance of her mother. But she did not want to make things worse, so she would stay in the hotel for the rest of the days reserved for the honeymoon.

The day could not have turned out worse. Manolo, in a moment of lucidity, approached his wife to try to make things right:

"I beg you to forgive me. I realize how unbalanced I've been. However, I am not to be blamed for what happened. That poor woman had obviously been following us. I got rid of her long before we were married. Just like other addicts, I had a sexual relationship with her. I tried to end the relationship honorably, including paying her for her sexual favors. Of course I wasn't going to tell you about my abominable conduct back then. I had no idea about the excellence of love, which for me had always entailed desire, pleasure and frustration."

After a few seconds of silence, he continued emotionally:

"I don't want to lose you because of the past. We have the present and the future to make our life together worthwhile and happy. If you can understand and forgive me, I'll be so grateful."

His eyes were misty and his voice less arrogant.

Eneida realized that this was a fundamental moment in their marriage, and although she felt hurt, she took her husband' cold, sweaty hands and responded tenderly:

"I love you so much that I felt like I was falling down a high mountain into a bottomless pit... Spinning round and round without support; I just wanted to disappear forever or go home, where I always felt safe."

She paused for a moment, and then went on:

"What's happening to us? What evil have we done in our lives to be persecuted like this, when all we want is to be happy? I feel that something or someone we can't see is provoking our failures the last two days, after the joys of our wedding. I know you may not be open to it, but I think we should pray, since we both believe in God and have religious faith."

Invited directly to communion with God, Manolo, who claimed to be a devout Catholic – but was only one socially – wanted to avoid it with an excuse. Eneida insisted, however, and then uttered a heartfelt prayer expressing grievances, hopes and petitions to God.

No prayer to the Father goes without an immediate response. In answer, venerable spirit friends approached the couple and enveloped them in a mild psychosphere, diluting the perverse and unhealthy vibrations that tried to dominate them, and causing them to enter a state of pleasant torpor, which eventually induced them to a special sleep.

During the trance of physiological sleep, Eneida felt herself leave her body for the first time and was able to benefit from the august, gentle presence of a female spirit haloed in an extraordinary light, who said to her in a kind but energetic tone:

"You have begun a long period of sublimation. Be careful about what you think and do. Envelop your husband in continuous waves of peace, and be patient and compassionate... You are both highly indebted to the people of South Africa because of wrongs you committed against them in the past. It is time to make reparations.

"Come with me!"

She took Eneida by the hand and they floated through the air, arriving at a cheerful, verdant landscape cut by the Vaal River.

At a certain distance, hovering in the air, she motioned with her right hand and, as if by magic, terrible scenes of war, cruelty and destruction ensued... The Whites, dominated by the fury of the most heinous passions, were slaughtering the autochthons, who were trying to keep them from advancing through their lands. Eneida watched as one of the Dutch conquerors and his wife furiously massacred children, the elderly and whoever got in their way. In the fury of battle, she suddenly saw the field strewn with corpses, which were piled up and burned, while the hordes of wicked foreigners continued on, hungry with ambition to consume the country's riches...

Soon afterward, everything returned to normal, to the silence of nature, broken by the sound of the meandering river and the soft breeze that the day was spreading before the burning sun.

Eneida was led back to her bed, where she began to awaken, still hearing the tender voice telling her:

"Now put on the *armor of faith* and the *helmet of courage,* equipping yourself with much love in order to overcome your afflictions. We will not leave you alone, and whenever you seek us through prayer, we will answer you."

Eneida woke up filled with profound inner joy, as if she had been released from a heavy load of afflictions. Manolo was filled with emotion when she told him about the dream, in which she felt she had been visited by some angelic being who was ready to help them on the journey they had just begun together.

From that moment on, a special calm hovered over the pair as they sensed the joy and expectations of future blessings.

With the honeymoon over, they returned to V., where their families were waiting joyously.

They had arranged to welcome them with an intimate meal in the couple's own home, where their mothers had unwrapped the gifts and arrayed them in one of the bedrooms to make it easier to admire them. The cards were attached to them so that the couple could thank the kind friends who had given them.

The magnificent residence, as well as the diamond necklace and earrings he had bought, must have depleted Manolo's savings, but that did not seem to matter much to him – he would deal with it later. At the moment he was interested in the celebrations and in enjoying all the sensations and emotions with which life was toasting him.

While Manolo's father's business was basically robbing the employees – mostly autochthons and a few immigrants – through unjust wages and a heavy burden of sacrifice in the parts foundries, the family, in its extravagance, spent huge sums on futilities and self-promotion.

Social injustice seems to be part of human beings, especially those who judge their neighbors according to their economic position, origin, race, beliefs, and political position. For a large slice of White society, the poor, the Blacks, the Indians, the Asians, and the uneducated are an unpleasant burden, from whom they would like to free themselves. Their presence makes them uneasy. However, nothing is done to advance them. They are kept in the fetters of moral misery and all its manifestations in order to continue to subject them and use them with scorn and disinterest.

However, the ferment of the hatred produced by the situation causes the masses to become increasingly aggressive – also perverse in its turn – in an unconscious form of retaliation, just waiting for the right time to erupt in hatred and horror. That is why ingratitude spreads, disrespect looms large and evil prevails.

Nevertheless, the Law of Progress is imposed by God, and no one can hold it back. Through historical and social processes, the phenomena of human renewal operate through missionaries and heroes, who appear from time to time, to influence thought, or through bloody civil wars, perverse guerrilla wars, and wars between and against nations... Rebelliousness is followed by insane and devastating violence.

Manolo, having been caught under the spell of putting on a wedding that was beyond his economic means, and in a way that would display a power that he was far from possessing, had compromised himself severely.

Such human folly, which derives from unhealthy pride, causes the absurdities that people find themselves beset with in the future, when debts that must be paid come due, but for which funds are unavailable, initiating internal and external disturbances that consume personal peace and social balance.

Consequently, Manolo had fallen into the trap of a shrewd, extortionate and powerful Portuguese moneylender, known to the community, who would become his merciless creditor.

But for now, all such worries would have to be postponed so that nothing would complicate the period of joyous pleasures.

The reception, therefore, was held with special care that thrilled the honorees. Only a few, carefully screened guests and noisy, deluded relatives had been invited to the tasteful love feast.

Normality slowly returned to the families, who seemed pleased by the tightening bonds of friendship.

A month or so had elapsed, when the country was rocked by a rebellion in the city of Soweto, in Johannesburg, and which was cruelly confronted and crushed by the government.

The prevailing misery had become too much to bear: hunger, drugs, prostitution, disease, and the indifference of the Whites, who did not even suspect the misery suffered by their black-skinned brethren, whose rights they were denying. It was a powder keg that blew up once again, but with more impact than on previous occasions...

The police reaction shook the world due to the display of cruelty and perversity of the well-equipped representatives of the law – of which law? The human one, obviously – compared to the rocks, pieces of wood and Molotov cocktails thrown by the desperate children, adolescents, women and men. As a consequence, the number of prisoners, dead and wounded went beyond the most pessimistic expectations.

The situation would no longer be the same from then on, due to resentment and ill-contained hatred.

Humanity's ideals are never crushed without resurfacing even more gravely and hatefully as a result of the harmful effects in which they originate as a result of the cruelty of those who repress them.

Apartheid would no longer mean exclusion for separate, false development, but would be a reaction of Blacks against Whites, of natives against invaders, of the natives' language against that of the foreigners, of the natives' beliefs against those imposed on them by the arrogance of the impious.

Naturally, the damaging results of the event spread through the settlements and the excluded peoples residing in their shameful ghettos.

The imposed mechanisms of communication were only used when absolutely necessary.

Although they had been divided by ethnicities, preventing better results against the arbitrary dominators, due to the prevalence of age-old hatreds, which continued to erupt into heinous crimes and mindless persecutions, they now felt the need to unite against their common enemy for the future results of the common good.

Those who had come from Mozambique and other border countries to compete for work in coal, gold, diamond and uranium mines were also discriminated against and persecuted. Attempts were made to prevent them from staying, because, in the myopia of the locals, they were competitors who would replace them, despite the widespread effects of asbestosis and silicosis, which were destroying numerous lives, dampening any sentiments of humanity or even compassion on the part of the employers.

As a means of revenge, many individuals who were discriminated against and possessed of a heinous moral complexion used the false pretext to commit robberies, assaults and murders, which were seldom solved, although capital punishment by hanging was enforced in the city of Pretoria.

While the Albuquerque family's economic affluence was on the rise, and they were thinking about starting their own business, the Rodriguez's, on the other hand, were transferring their money to Spain because they were planning to eventually abandon the generous lands that had welcomed and prospered them.

They frequently used recondite resources to send large sums of money in gold coins – krugerrands – or in Rands, the national currency – for deposit in special bank accounts and safes of their home country.

By the third month of marriage, the young Spaniard did not try to hide a certain amount of boredom concerning the life he was leading. He stopped visiting the Latin club, as would be normal, because he no longer felt the need for entertainment. After all, the home should be the reason for his happiness; still, some friends prone to parties and delusion urged him so strongly that he returned to attend a celebration one Saturday night.

After convincing his young wife that he himself could not miss the celebration, but that it was not advisable for her to be there, he set off in the direction of happiness like a bird freed from its golden but stifling cage, anticipating the pleasure he would *re-experience* to the maximum. The so-called surprises of the unknown always pleased him in a special way, and to experience them once again was one of life's real rewards.

The extravagant celebration was regarding the election of the club's new managers, who intended to make it exclusive, reserved solely for the arrogant owners of the country. This obviously revealed the conflict of inferiority they felt before other individuals who could not hide their contempt for them.

Thus, after the celebration amongst applause and jubilation, appetizers gave way to unbridled drunkenness, and the normally agreeable dancing became a spectacle of the turmoil of the passions.

Next, the overflowing of sensuality exploded into licentiousness, transforming the familiar and social environment, forcing the more-responsible individuals to leave, those who could not condone the extravagances and excesses of the pseudo-rich and their lust.

Manolo began the trip back to the primitive behavior of his pre-marriage days and let himself be carried away by the disruptive chaos. Only very early in the morning, when dawn was preparing to defeat the night, did he resolve, almost intoxicated, to return home.

He had a hard time driving and was guided more by instinct than by lucidity. As he approached his residence, he noticed some figures moving in his direction, motioning him to stop. In a flash he realized it might be a trap. Dazed, he drove toward the figures in a delusional attempt to free himself, but instead crashed into a tree standing in the way.

He was injured when his head hit the steering wheel, and when he tried to stagger out, two dreadful-looking men approached and began beating him. They seemed to know him, and in their native language they unleashed their anger, just stopping short of killing him.

Fortunately, another night owl driving in the same direction saw what was happening and began honking his horn. The assailants fled and the man stopped and got out to offer Manolo first aid before taking him to the nearest hospital.

Eneida was awake at home, waiting for her husband. When he did not return, she was filled with dread and perceived that something terrible had happened. Very early in the morning, tired from a lack of sleep, she called the Albuquerques, who found out that Manolo was still unconscious in the hospital's ICU, the victim of a concussion.

The person who had rescued him left notes about what he had witnessed and stated that he was available for any clarifications that might be necessary.

Consequently, it was easy for both families to learn of the disastrous event and take the necessary measures with the police so that the miscreants would be identified and punished.

Overcome with grief, Eneida arrived at the hospital. She was not allowed to see Manolo yet and had to wait in a special room for news as to whether or not he would live.

The families were shocked by what had happened. It was not unprecedented, because such events had been occurring in different parts of the country, especially in the Transvaal region, which was more at the center of the political and racial unrest.

Youthful strength and close medical monitoring succeeded in bringing the patient out of the coma, and he was transferred to an Intermediate Care Unit, enabling his wife and relatives to visit him. Manolo was extremely weak due to the loss of blood and the trauma from the blows, and could not remember exactly how everything had happened. Unfortunately, he did remember the face of one of the attackers – the one who seemed more merciless – as being a recently fired employee who had vowed revenge... But everything in his memory was still vague, imprecise...

Surrounded by the affection of his family and the specialized devotion of the medical team, two weeks later he was well-settled in a comfortable room in the same hospital, where he quickly recovered.

Instead of his formerly aggressive temperament, he was now withdrawn, silent for long periods, even when invited to take part in conversations. He avoided them, whereas he had been loquacious and talkative.

Eneida tried unsuccessfully to distract him from the bitter memory of that awful night.

God, however, reduced the burden of their afflictions and provided a happy solution. Eneida, now in the fourth month of marriage, found out she was pregnant, and the news was conveyed with joy to her husband, who could not conceal his happiness.

The surprise was such that he allowed himself to be overcome by great euphoria, drawing his wife into an affectionate embrace and giving her an effusive kiss of gratitude and love.

He had never really imagined himself as a father, despite his immense desire to be one. Thus, in his characteristically enthusiastic behavior, he subjected Eneida to a lot of questions and urged her to rest and to take special care of herself. It was his way of showing his happiness, lessening the impact of the cowardly assault of which he had been the victim.

Now, at last, new directions were being drawn for the future of the Rodriguez family.

4
WILD PASSIONS AND HAPPY OPPORTUNITIES

The days were spent on the patient's recovery, which now involved a long period of convalescence in the privacy of his lovely home.

Even though Manolo was happy at the prospect of being a father, he could not hide the rancor that gripped him regarding the assault. He was devising a way of getting even with the thug who had so cowardly attacked him, accompanied by another criminal.

He could vaguely recall the fired employee and was soon able to contact other workers from his company, asking one of them, who was fond of him, to pay him a visit. He took the opportunity to offer him a generous reward if he discovered the whereabouts of his enemy and confirm the crime of which he suspected him.

Since individuals are usually unable to keep still, the assailant had been bragging about it and betraying himself. Hence it did not take long for his identity to reach his former boss's informant.

Instead of reporting it to the competent authorities, Manolo designed a plan for revenge, which he would carry out as soon as the circumstances permitted.

Let us explain that Mr. Giménez Rodríguez and his wife Santiaga were from the island of Majorca or Mallorca, in the Balearics east of Spain. Being one of the largest in the archipelago, its capital, Palma de Mallorca, is visited by international tourists due to its pleasant climate and geographical position. The Rodríguez's were born there into a modest clan. Their children were also born there, and were brought to South Africa as children, putting down roots there, like many others, in hopes of gainful employment, which they finally found.

Now, Giménez yearned to return to his native city if he could sell his business – a business he had not always engaged in honestly – which he intended to do as soon as possible. He had already benefitted from the company's best results and now he feared the growing wave of discontent of the Blacks, who rightfully yearned to retake possession of their land, their nation.

Since he traveled periodically with his wife to Spain, and then on to his birthplace, after the unfortunate events involving Manolo, he was on an extended journey of relaxation in preparation for the final move.

Although Manolo was still recovering, the business was left in his care, and even from bed, he was able to manage the metallurgical foundry well.

Now, however, as the months passed and the bills arrived, swollen by exorbitant interest, Manolo's bad mood increased, as he was plagued by debts that he could not liquidate. Among the creditors hounding him, the worst one was a loan shark called "the Portuguese," as if he did not have an actual name. He was feared because of his arbitrariness and dishonesty, especially with regard to the way he transferred currencies and laundered money through deposits abroad. He knew the character of many who were harming the country, and did not hide from anyone his propensity to act as a "stool pigeon" if his loans and services were not paid for as agreed at the time of the negotiations.

On the other hand, regarding the Albuquerques, Henrique's wife and children had come from the city of Luanda, the beautiful former capital of Angola, whereas the doctor, himself, was born in the north of Portugal, where he completed his studies at the venerable University of Coimbra. He was fluent in several languages and was highly interested in philosophy and religion. In spite of the distressing situation in which he had arrived in the new country, he, too, longed to return to his homeland. He could use his immense potential and be useful in the political and social transformations that Portugal was undergoing. Nevertheless, he understood that that would only be possible in the future when his economic and financial situation was more secure. Of course, he also feared the situation in South Africa, and so he transferred any and all acquired resources to Portugal, where he planned to end his days of physical existence with his family.

Eneida's marriage was a pleasant surprise because he realized that his adopted daughter would not have to work. She could live quite affluently in the company of her chosen one.

Of course, being unable to peer into the arcana of fate, he could never have imagined the tragedies and suffering that would come later, altering his and his family's plans for happiness.

It is worth mentioning that a certain calm apparently reigned over their respective families.

Manolo gradually retook the reins of managing the family business, and could now go to the office...

Of course, he was not the same. The blows to his head probably affected his mental and emotional behavior, which was already unstable before the event.

His persistent idea for revenge enabled him to organize a group of employees who captured the assailant. That night they brought him to the company's headquarters, where he was severely punished by his captors and by Manolo himself, who did not hesitate to get even, threatening to kill him if he ever met him again anywhere at any time. Moreover, Manolo promised an even worse corrigendum if he decided to turn him over to the police with "special instructions."

The poor man endured the ordeal and was thrown out of the city limits, totally beaten up. Without medical assistance, he discarnated in a pitiful state of rancor and hatred.

Almost no one noticed he was missing. His body was discovered accidentally by passersby when it was in cadaveric decomposition, and the crime did not arouse much interest in the police authorities, who were used to the nefarious processes of *justice at one's own hands,* now common throughout the country.

Although the criminal and his thugs went unpunished, Manolo's heinous crime would weigh heavily on his irresponsible conscience from then on.

Moreover, his behavioral disorder had not disappeared, inducing him to resume his alcoholism, which neither his wife nor family could prevent.

On the couple's wedding anniversary, Manolo, still in the grips of his vanity, demanded that Eneida wear the diamond necklace and earrings, demonstrating the fascination the jewels had over him. Eneida's due date was approaching and she looked radiant with the splendor that maternity gives women, adorning them with special beauty.

Even though the anniversary celebration was tiring for Eneida in her advanced condition, it was a reward and a joy, which had been scarce in the home, and a pleasant get-together with the family members, slowly being alienated by Manolo, who displayed his moral deficiency in the form of jealousy.

It was true that he willingly offered all the material comfort possible to his wife, but he had become aggressive and hard to deal with, except when he was stimulated by alcohol, when he would become overly enthusiastic, almost irreverent and inopportune.

Júlio, the patient brother-in-law, managed to gain Manolo's friendship, although he often needed to oppose the latter's irrational reactions. He, too, was young and thus became a pleasing companion for the couple, without arousing Manolo's habitual resentment. Consequently, he would sometimes play golf or cards with him, or go to the swimming pool, where they enjoyed each other's company. Eneida, on the other hand, was unable to enjoy such pleasures because of her pregnancy, but once in a while, she would accompany them, protecting herself at a distance, slowly realizing her disoriented partner's emotional withdrawal.

Manolo was restless and saw himself as a true *Latin lover,* allowing himself frivolities incompatible with his marital commitment.

Influenced by alcohol, on one of these outings he mentioned how he had avenged himself by punishing the thug who had assaulted him in the darkness. He did not know about the final consequences of his equally cowardly act, but that fact did not justify his having committed it.

As soon as he had completed a period of spiritual torment, the victim, N'Bondo, crazed with hatred, was psychically drawn to the one responsible for his death, thus became part of the wretched group of discarnates who surrounded Manolo, waiting for the opportunity for lamentable processes of spiritual revenge.

N'Bondo was a Zulu descendent and, like thousands of others, was in the region in search of a better quality of life, residing in a miserable area on the outskirts of the city, without hygiene, running water or sewage. He did not live in a house, but in the saddest poverty in an infested hut with his wife and three young children. At first, his disappearance was seen as an escape from family responsibilities, as was always the case. The matter was only clarified later when the corpse, with great difficulty, could be identified by the poor widow, adding to the misery and abandonment she was now experiencing because of N'Bondo's disappearance. He had definitely not been someone with character or moral principles; instead, as a result of his existence, he had become an alcoholic, spending what little money he made on what was essential for his family and his addiction...

Such is undoubtedly one of the worst consequences of moral misery: the total lack of interest in a better existence, of changes to higher levels of behavior, where one can experience less hardship. Poverty, the absence of any stimuli and expectations for a better situation, keep human beings at a lower level, where they are disinterested in accomplishing anything more than meeting the immediacy of the daily routine: eating, sleeping, having sex, getting drunk, in a search for a little pleasure to diminish the harshness in which they struggle.

The days are still far off, when earthly social justice will finally understand that happiness is the result of the unity of human sentiments for the common good, and that as long as there is a disregard for one's neighbors and indifference toward their needs, disorder, insanity and suffering will reign supreme.

The advancement of the various areas of knowledge demonstrates that evolution is a collective process involving all individuals, who must help one another other for the common cause. Fortunately, such aspirations are already being experienced via multiple movements, which call on governments and citizens to change their perspective on life and its existential purposes.

As Manolo euphorically told him about the beating he had inflicted on N'Bondo, Júlio could not help but feel repulsed by his venal and proud brother-in-law. Discovering this facet of his behavior, which money had helped to develop, he began to fear for his sister's safety. He now understood that she had married an aggressive, dissimulative psychopath.

An irrational braggart par excellence, the half-drunk openly exposed himself to his almost terrified brother-in-law, without, of course, realizing the confession he was making.

Still in the paroxysm of drunkenness, he blurted out that he was providing a timely blow against the heinous society he detested, and for that very reason, he had bought the diamond necklace and earrings for his wife out of love, but also as a precautionary measure for the future... He could not hide the fascination that those stones exerted on his greed, but he lamented the high sum that he would still have to pay to become their real owner.

Because he continued with his guilty conscience-releasing narratives, he kept on drinking until he passed out, requiring Júlio to take him home.

Júlio could not get over his astonishment, so that same night he narrated the occurrence to his mother and stepfather, revealing part of Manolo's dark and degrading landscape and wondering how to protect his sister in the future. The future, however, is unpredictable and often comes before the present has completed its schedule...

The birth of little Esperanza was a blessing in the Rodríguez home because it was able to reunite families that had become somewhat distanced. After the celebrations in the hospital where the natural childbirth had occurred, mother and daughter were welcomed home by the little darling's joyous grandparents, aunts and uncles.

Esperanza was a docile spirit, the bearer of expressive moral values, but still possessing a heavy load of moral debts to pay. Her arrival on earth had been lovingly prepared so that she could redeem past wrongs while at the same time making room so that the hearts that surrounded her in the home could lay down safety guidelines for the future.

However, human beings do not always submit to the divine designs, penetrating into the hidden meaning of occurrences in order to derive from them the most benefit, which is always the result of experience and enlightening events.

It is wrongly believed that one's physical life must always transpire in a climate of euphoria and joy, rather than in illness, failure, anguish, death... Human beings have not yet acknowledged the transience of the physical vehicle, so they do not reflect deeply regarding the spiritual process of evolution. They long for pleasure, as if there were no other values to be experienced, and for things to be easy, as if everything should transpire in a springtime climate, despite disasters of every order, which derive from the passions, the base sentiments and selfishness, with all its minions. If they would behave rationally and obey the Natural Laws of the Universe, they would not stumble over the moral disasters that unfold while they are busy taking care of their own personal interests to the exclusion of those that concern others.

Only awareness of personal and collective responsibility concerning life will grant a measure of equanimity for less-distressing behavior and a more feasible walk with happiness.

Little Esperanza managed to arouse feelings in her father that he did not know he had. Because of his macho culture, he had wanted a son, and at first he was disappointed with the birth of a girl. Nevertheless, after seeing her and feeling her in his lap, his disappointment was completely overcome and he could not hide the thrill of happiness that assailed him. The child's presence became a breeze of peace in the heat of the conflicts that plagued the helter-skelter being that was Manolo.

One could understand how the newborn's sweetness, her complete dependence, and her fragility constituted an instrument of security for the troubled father, who consequently felt indispensable and powerful, bearing the values that would protect the child from the hostile world and wicked people.

In the inebriation of the senses, believing happiness to be an unending string of joys and pleasures, Manolo began surrounding Eneida with the affection that he had denied her of late.

About a month after Esperanza's birth, he came up with the idea of holding a baptism party, faithful to the traditions of his religious faith. The event would take place in an atmosphere of great emotion and festivity, with relatives on both sides and very few friends being invited to a commemorative dinner at his residence. He seemed desirous of reestablishing bonds of friendship and understanding, indispensable for the maintenance of a harmonious social group.

On the appointed day and time, while the guests helped themselves to soft drinks, whiskey and canapés, Manolo asked Eneida, a fairly accomplished pianist, to treat everyone with a number on the piano.

Since they had gotten married, she only played it once in a while in order not to lose her ability.

The guests nodded effusively, and after they were all seated in the large room, whose wide doors opened out toward a well-designed garden, she modestly prepared for the performance.

It was February, and a cold wind was blowing, but the special group found it to be pleasant.

It was a lovely evening. The sky was dotted with stars, and a dazzling moon enveloped the earth in silver. The lazy, winding Vaal River glided gently along, while the breeze bore from afar the sounds of the wretched residents in the shantytowns of the suburbs.

Taken with poetic inspiration, Eneida began playing Beethoven's *Moonlight Sonata,* flooding the room and surroundings with poetic, descriptive music.

Manolo, strongly impressed, took a silver three-arm candelabrum fit with slender candles, lit them, placed it on the piano, and turned off the electric light.

The environment was charged with unusual vibrations that affected the audience.

The young pianist seemed endowed with a strange spiritual force that enabled her to duplicate the moving scene when the noted composer wrote the score and then played the piece so that a blind woman, who had asked him what a moonlit night was like, could get an idea of the majesty of Selene reigning in the star-filled canopy.

Human creatures often need moments of beauty and reflection in order to tune in to the love that shines everywhere. In the hustle and bustle of unnecessary pursuits, and in the exhausting demands of the lower passions, they lose touch with their own reality. They take extraordinary measures to acquire things and forget their responsibilities and duties, anesthetizing their sentiments, disguising occurrences, and experiencing shameful, exhausting pleasures.

Any incident that induces one to meditate, to go inside, to halt the unbridled race of the five senses promotes the tenderness, the encounter with inner harmony, the inner satisfaction and the well-being that contribute to one's emotional and spiritual renewal.

It is regrettable, however, that such moments are rare in families that seldom get together, and when they do get together, it is almost always for aggressive arguments, tormenting excuses, and undue accusations.

When the home finally becomes a stronghold of love and when those in it feel a need to help each other, there will be a radical change of behavior in non-consanguineous social groups, in work places and everywhere else, because, harmonized within, individuals will always be in tune with life, radiating this valuable achievement.

When Eneida finished the piece, there was a long silence. No applause, which would be unnecessary and would break the majesty of the moment.

Still enveloped by the same élan, she glided her fingers over the keyboard and began playing Schubert's *Ave Maria,* which enveloped the friends and family in waves of magical tenderness.

In that spiritual, almost sacred atmosphere, the soprano voice of Manolo's sister, Margarita, joined in to complement the incomparable piece, extolling the Mother of the Nazarene in the song's traditional Latin.

Without their realizing it, the eyes of the audience became moist with tears and they felt the joy of true communion with Immortality, because benevolent spirits had come and enveloped all of them in their kindly vibrations of peace and hope.

When it was over and the lights were turned back on, spontaneous, rousing applause crowned the improvised spectacle.

At that moment, the butler invited them all to dinner, which was served in an adjoining room, meeting the rigors and demands of the *nouveaux riches.*

Four tables, with seats for four people each, had been placed around the central table, which was decorated with an embroidered white linen tablecloth from the island of Madeira. Adding to the environment were two silver candlesticks with lighted candles on the table, and in the center were fresh flowers with a few beautiful, native protea mixed in. The elaborate sterling silver tableware, the place settings and the fine Sevres crystal bore the couple's initials, characterizing good taste and refinement.

The courses of the sumptuous dinner followed. Right after the appetizers, accompanied by fine red wine, the hot dishes were served, featuring lentil soup, pheasant and cordon-bleu, with rice, mashed potatoes and other complements.

The wines varied according to the requirement of each real or imaginary enologist. Then came chocolate mousse, fruit mousse, ice cream, some of which had been flambéed. The lavish banquet ended with glasses of cognac, and cups of coffee and tea from China.

The guests were smitten by the excellence of the meal, and the gentlemen kept talking about the quality and refinement of the reception as they puffed smoke into the air, denoting their self-satisfaction. The women, in turn, also praised the good taste of Eneida and Manolo honoring, in such a way, little Esperanza, who was now considered to be Christian, having been baptized that morning, thereby becoming part of the new society.

In this atmosphere of emotion and jubilation, the guests began to say goodbye while the dreamy and mysterious night dominated nature.

5

DARKNESS THICKENS OVER DESTINIES

Inter-pocula[7], events took place in an apparently balanced way, which would not lead one to believe, or even to imagine, that a massive river of sludge was running beneath the surface, because, in order to maintain his self-attributed *status*, Manolo began to divert funds from the company, thus harming it, without the family realizing it, although they would before long, of course. At the same time, he began to take out more loans with *the Portuguese*, who, like a merciless bird of prey, charged interest that was more and more exorbitant.

For any greedy moneylender, the more complicated the life of the client, the better the reaping of the fruits of the heinous business.

Since the debt was already significant, amounting to a total of some tens of thousands of rands, the ambitious and unscrupulous creditor suggested to the rash young man that he pay down a good part of it, thereby avoiding the accumulation of interest, which would certainly land him in a painful situation.

---

7   Literally "between cups"; of an intimate character (Spirit Author).

The truth, however, is that the Portuguese knew that the Rodríguez's company was in a somewhat dangerous situation, as were all industrial and commercial enterprises in those difficult days of insecurity.

Due to Manolo's arrogant temperament, when the exploiter made the proposal, denoting a lack of trust, an altercation was unavoidable. The moneylender felt disrespected, wounded in his honor, because he was attributing moral qualities to himself that he did not really possess. He stated angrily:

"After all, extravagant parties can only be hosted by those who are capable of it. You won't succeed in using the money I have loaned you to maintain an enviable but completely fake state of affairs."

The Portuguese displayed both arrogance and impertinence. He had not yet been harmed by his client, revealing, perhaps unwittingly, that he envied the pleasures Manolo was allowing himself. Likewise, neither one had any liking for the other; on the contrary, there was well disguised, inexplicable animosity.

Manolo retorted bluntly:

"Your profession is just pitiable. It repeats the evil deed of Judas, cursed through the millennia. I do what I feel is best in my life, and I won't let you get in the way. After all, the money I get from you, for which you extract the very last drop of blood from my work, isn't yours anymore the moment I reward you with the exorbitant interest you charge."

"Don't forget I warned you! I expect you to fail, but I won't be a victim of the fraudulent bankruptcy you're constructing for yourself. I'll get my money back no matter what, so don't play around with me," snorted the cynical and hateful creditor.

"I never neglect my responsibilities, especially when it comes to the dregs of society that you are," replied the Spaniard with the same audacity.

Their moral behavior was on the same level, which is why they did business together. Their inferior interests produced identical spiritual vibrations.

"No doubt," said the collector, "the rabble only exists in society because society maintains it. That's our situation. Without you, I couldn't survive. But without me, you'd be wallowing in the mud you came from. Keep in mind that your debt now adds up to the value of that necklace and earrings. They rightfully belong to me, and they could easily pay off all your debt if you had the dignity to acknowledge how boastful but poor you really are."

The offense was too much. After a nervous, ironic and somewhat crazed laugh, Manolo exploded:

"Oh, now I get it! You're so greedy that you want the diamond necklace and earrings for yourself! ... Well, you'll never get them. Even if it looks like I'm going to go completely broke, I would rather toss them in the ocean than hand them over to a wretch like you."

Shaking all over, the young man stood up behind his desk, shoved his chair violently, and with a threatening look, he advanced as if he were going to punch the Portuguese, who instinctively turned away and shouted:

"I'll be back, maybe sooner than you think to unmask you, you fake!"

He stormed out, as if deranged.

Manolo yelled at the top of his lungs:

"I'll be waiting. Do your worst, coward!"

The totally inexplicable incident unnerved Manolo. He knew the usurer was ruthless, but he knew that he had been making the monthly payments on the promissory notes he had signed, and, without understanding what had actually happened, he concluded that it was the Portuguese's ambition to get the diamonds, which were definitely worth a fortune. He himself had acquired them while thinking of possible hard times ahead, and that it would be easy to take them abroad and sell them for a good price.

After arriving at this conclusion, Manolo was overcome with rage. Since he was incapable of handling natural conflicts resulting from any kind of struggle, he opened a cupboard in the office and poured a good dose of whisky to calm himself down, but he only felt even more confused for the rest of the day.

When he arrived home for dinner, the vexation assailing him was visible on his face and in his behavior. Since he had not told his wife about the debt he had been piling up, Eneida had no idea of the unfortunate incidents he had been experiencing. Nevertheless, perceiving that he was upset, she tried to cheer him up. She put Esperanza on his lap, which always calmed him down when any kind of torment afflicted him.

It was the perfect solution, because after just a few minutes, he was a new man. He accepted Eneida's suggestion to shower and relax before dinner.

He would have forgotten all about the incident with the Portuguese, were it not for a tragic event that would take place a few days later.

Due to his job as a businessman and keeper of assets, Manolo had obtained permission from the police to carry a gun in case he had to defend himself in some dangerous situation. The country was going through seriously perilous times involving assaults, robberies and other violent crimes... Thus, with Eneida's knowledge, he also kept a loaded revolver in the drawer of the nightstand in case of an emergency. Despite the strength of the building itself, plus the security cameras and the watchman, the measure with the gun was precautionary, as practiced by nearly all the most affluent people.

Late one night, Manolo heard suspicious noises in the room. Without turning on the light, he saw two figures sneak out from behind the curtains and move toward the closet where the jewels, coins, and private family documents were stored in a safe. The soft light coming through the large window through the sheer curtains made it possible to make out the shadowy figures that slid open the door to the huge, built-in closet. Using a flashlight, one of them managed to pick the lock to the door, which gave way with some ease, and began to rummage through the clothes, exposing the safe...

Like a savage feline, Manolo, who was following the thief's action, carefully opened the drawer where the gun was located, and fired two shots. One hit the thief squarely and he fell in a puddle of blood. The other escaped, running and screaming...

Panic ensued. Eneida awoke in alarm; little Esperanza began crying; the night watchman came running; the lights came on, and the tragedy was consummated.

The thief lay on the floor with his hand to his chest. Blood was pouring out and he was moaning in unbearable pain.

While the watchman called the police, Manolo began slapping the thief without mercy, trying to make him confess. The poor man was unable to reason and could only ask for help in his dialect, afraid of his impending death. He passed out more than once, returning to despair. A police car arrived; the officers entered the luxurious residence, and reached the now bloody bedroom. An ambulance also arrived with doctors and assistants, who put the dying man on a stretcher to take him to the emergency room.

Manolo was completely upset, wondering what was happening to him, and when the wounded man was lifted up to the light, Manolo asked him:

"What were you looking for, you bastards? Who was your partner?"

In a delirium, the thief stammered:

"The diamonds!"

Like a flash of lightning, Manolo realized that this had been a plot forged by the infamous Portuguese, who had obviously hired the poor Blacks in his vain desire to get the precious stones and avenge himself for the argument they had had. With that disturbing thought, he tried to calm himself down, letting his excited imagination work out his own plan for revenge.

The stranger died on the way to the hospital, keeping the name of his partner secret, as well as other details.

The next day, Manolo was summoned to the police station to explain and justify what had happened. It was not considered a crime, because the thief was caught red-handed in the privacy of the bedroom.

After a preliminary hearing, a new one was set for later, when the process would be ended definitively.

The trauma resulting from the unfortunate event affected the whole family, who could not imagine something that bad happening in the privacy of the couple's home.

With her husband's permission, Eneida and little Esperanza went to spend a few days with her family while he cleaned up and replaced the blue carpet that had covered the bedroom floor.

The walls were repainted and some of the furniture was moved around, but the vestiges of the tragedy would remain an unpleasant memory for a long time.

Manolo, however, with the fixed idea about the origin of the theft, gave vent to his imagination, looking for the best way to get revenge.

The Portuguese was a delusional individual. He had come from Mozambique, where he had committed various moral and financial wrongs in Lourenço Marques. Consequently, he had practically been thrown out of town soon after the liberation of the colony. He had gone to South Africa with a wave of immigrants to give life there a try. Living at first in Johannesburg, then in Pretoria, neither locale had worked out for him, so he moved to the city where he now resided, and where, thanks to initial protection by some generous compatriots, he managed to save some money and find legal ways to transfer it to Portugal through an agency he gradually set up and used as a front to hide his heinous profession as a loan shark.

His rise in the business world was highly controversial. It was even said that he was also working in the trafficking of Mozambican immigrants, whom he *sold* to gold, coal and diamond miners. He demanded high fees from his victims to get them jobs – if such could be called free labor, instead of slavery – which exhausted its victims in a short time, while he himself received a generous cut from their new bosses. Thrown into veritable refugee camps, they were discriminated against by Whites and autochthones alike, and were housed in separate barracks, suffering general persecution.

Moreover, it was said that, in order to collect his extortionate interest, he did not hesitate to have those who did not repay their debts eliminated by hiring a few miserable Mozambicans, whom he exploited mercilessly, forcing them to live on the wages of evil while receiving crumbs as their recompense.

Having reached a state of economic independence, he was sought by his compatriots, who wanted to illegally transfer money, gold coins and other assets to Portugal out of fear of the much talked about revolution. However, he was not respected by them – exploiters, the tormenters society, never are. They are accepted and feared, but are never loved or taken into account. They are a moral scourge that brands them irreversibly as detestable. Their fortune is always pitiful because it is made with the sweat and tears of the many who have been crushed by the circumstances by which they have benefited.

Human beings cannot escape their mental aspirations and ambitions of any nature. According to the structure of their thoughts and sentiments, the characteristics of the hidden being who they really are is made clear by their behavior.

The Portuguese had married when he was in Mozambique but was widowed a few years later, although it was said at the time that he had been a fraudulent widower, implying that he had been responsible for the death of his wife due to an extramarital affair with the woman who now shared his tortuous existence. He had not had children, which made him even crueler. Hence he had never known the tenderness of fatherhood and thus could not understand the meaning of procreation, through which the sentiment of love increases, reaching high levels of happiness.

He had won many enemies, who wished him dead – a happy solution to many debts difficult to redeem. More than once, clients had filed complaints against him so that his wickedness would not continue outside the law and justice.

But let's be frank: although the authorities knew about his behavior, he had the monetary resources to keep them quiet. In short, the death of the life-sucking vampire would have been a blessing to lives put on hold.

The Portuguese, of course, was highly cautious. He was a master of his craft, which he recognized to be dangerous, and for that very reason he was accompanied by discreet friends, who in reality were his truculent bodyguards. "The Portuguese" was the epithet that his friends had given him, but his legal name was Antônio Manuel de Alcântara e Silva, born in a small village near Bragança, in a county in the province of Trás-os-Montes and Alto Douro...

6
THE UNLEASHING OF A NEW TRAGEDY

Despite being tormented and often out of control, Manolo was at times seized by impulses of generosity, which gave a different impression to his character.

The practice of the good is always worthwhile in any form, for it confers positive dividends on the doer.

Among the foundry's employees, one, named Mayuso, had held an immense debt of gratitude to his boss. Months earlier, his little girl, living in a situation of misery and malnutrition, had gotten very sick with pneumonia. Mayuso was unable to put her in the hospital, so he asked Manolo for help. Manolo felt sorry for him and mobilized resources and friends. The child was admitted to the hospital and immediately placed in a safe, comfortable bed. She was only ten years old and would have died had it not been for the lifesaving measure. Two weeks later, she had recovered, was discharged, and allowed to return without embarrassment or difficulty to her simple home on the outskirts of the city. Manolo himself took her there and was appalled by the family's misery.

The next day, he called Mayuso into his office and offered him financial resources so that the girl would lack nothing, and the family's miserable situation would be mitigated.

Taken with amazement at this unusual generosity, Mayuso thanked Manolo by kissing his hand in a gesture of deep humility, and assuring him:

"Boss, from now on you do not have just an employee; you have a slave, who will spare no effort to serve you, even with his very life."

Tears streamed down his cheeks, and his eyes were bloodshot with emotion.

The intensity of the scene impressed Manolo, producing a feeling of unspeakable well-being. The joy of doing the good is like precious nectar, giving uncontained pleasure.

Now, after the incident with the Portuguese, Manolo had begun to act very strangely, characterized by a more-pronounced anger and revolt that generated a lot of comments.

One evening at the end of the workday, Mayuso asked Manolo if he could speak with him. He went on to explain:

"I know something very troubling has been afflicting the Boss. Of course, it's a private matter and none of my business, but I want to remind you that I will always be at your side, especially when it comes to taking care of any problem when no one else can, not even the Boss himself."

After a pause, during which Manolo remained silent, he continued:

"Everything gets known, one way or another. They say that another white man of Portuguese nationality, a loan shark and scoundrel, is mocking and disrespecting the Boss, trying to dishearten him ... Among us Kaffirs, when someone talks a lot and says what isn't true, the attitude to be taken is to shut him up so that the others continue to respect the victim, and the matter is resolved honorably."

Angered by the information that his opponent was mocking his character, Manolo suppressed his revulsion and asked:

"Well, how might we silence the blabbermouth if he is always accompanied by others of the same carat?"

"By finding the best time and place. Without the Boss asking me, I decided, on my own, to find out about his behavior and habits. I found out that he has a relationship with a black woman, who acts as his mistress. She also came here from Mozambique and is a widow of one of those he brought here. He's always alone when he goes to see her. He stays until the wee hours of the morning, and then goes home as if nothing happened, a home he corrupts with his immoral behavior. If we are careful and precise, we will find an excellent opportunity to punish him." He laughed with natural, almost naive joy.

The Spaniard could not believe it; this was exactly what he was looking for. He said he needed time to think, to make plans. They would talk again at the first opportunity.

Manolo's mood had suddenly changed. He took his employee's hands and squeezed them as if sealing a very serious pact between the two of them.

Feeling honored for the opportunity to reciprocate the good he had received, unaware of what it meant, but proud of the opportunity to repay his employer, Mayuso went back to his hut singing to himself an old tribal song in his native language, evoking war and victory.

Gratitude is a very rare sentiment in the hearts of human creatures, who only think of receiving gifts or being served. They rarely repay gestures of love with the dimension with which they ought to be clothed. That is why animosities, indifference to pain and wounded emotions abound and give way to exorbitant and perverse individualism, preventing the advance of solidarity, which would open up immense spaces for flights of love.

Nevertheless, in the moral constitution of the humble black servant there was a treasure of gratitude, which, unfortunately, would become a sickle of unhappiness about to reap his life also. In pledging himself to his boss as he had, he knew the gravity of the commitment and its consequences, but in his way of looking at life, no sacrifice was sufficient to demonstrate the thankfulness that dominated his inner landscape.

Manolo was very pleasantly surprised by his employee's spontaneous offer and was beginning to look forward to the joys resulting from his tormenter's disappearance.

For his part, Mayuso would devote himself to monitoring the Portuguese's movements.

When he told Manolo that he planned to follow the enemy – that is how the Portuguese was to be defined – he asked him for a work schedule that would allow for greater freedom of movement, without the constriction of the clock. That way, he could learn the habits of the Portuguese and devise a plan for the treachery.

From then on, replicating the *law of the jungle*, the hungry lioness would follow the swift gazelle until the perfect time to catch it and reap its existence.

The Spaniard knew that the promissory notes his creditor had in his possession stated that he could demand payment whenever he wanted, although there was a gentlemen's commitment – if that is what it could be called – to do so only monthly. The money would not be put in the bank, thus avoiding any unpleasant explanations in the future by the Portuguese.

Less than a month had passed before it seemed that the Fates had given their nod to the soulless conspirators. Debtor and creditor met for a casual meeting, and instead of the moneylender trying to come across as aggressive or rancorous, he sought to be amicable and suggested that they reconcile. After all, they should see themselves as friends, perfectly capable of getting passed unfortunate arguments. Now was a good time *to shelve the resentment.* Manolo seemed to agree in good faith, but actually felt jubilant at this occurrence because it would open up possibilities for the consummation of his plan.

Prolonging the conversation, he said that, due to unexpected positive results at the company from a large government order, he might be able to pay off some of the notes.

The Portuguese's eyes gleamed with greed, and he asked:

"Wouldn't you really like to rid yourself of those diamonds? Now don't be angry at my question. We both have jewelry set aside for hard times. We could settle the whole business and free you from having to pay the whole amount plus the interest, which is always a heavy burden on any debt."

Stung with revulsion, but keeping his head, Manolo replied:

"I must confess I'll have to think about it," he said in a tone of humility and reflection. Once again, he could see that the nefarious Portuguese really had tried to rob him of the valuable stones, and in his unbridled fascination he still meant to do so.

Thus, Manolo proposed with apparent agreement:

"Come to my office the day after tomorrow after we've shut down. Bring your notes and the documents so that we can negotiate the complete settlement of the debt in an atmosphere of calm, without witnesses or interruptions by employees."

And maintaining his natural tone of voice, he explained:

"Needless to say, this is just between you and me. I won't tell my wife or other family members. When she looks for the necklace and the earrings, I'll tell her they must have been stolen after all by those bastards who invaded our bedroom – as you must have heard."

"Yes, yes," stammered the other. "I did hear about that, but I didn't give it much thought. After all, crime nowadays is embraced in desperation, causing insecurity and increasing the evil that has hit the country ever since it was conquered by the Europeans. It seems to me that the time has come when the Blacks are trying to get revenge on the slave drivers."

He was really cynical – thought Manolo, who was delighted at the Portuguese's embarrassment – for he had been the author of the attempted robbery that had resulted in the death of one of the thieves and the disappearance of the other. He probably knew where that one was, because he had lured him with his tricks and vileness.

Both were quite pleased – so it seemed, at least – and they shook hands, each thinking of how best to seal the fate of the other – with the stamp of cruelty, of course.

It was crystal clear that the Portuguese yearned for the possession of the jewels. They exerted a strange fascination over him, which surprised even him. Of course, he loved precious stones, gold and platinum – anything that might be of high value to soothe his unbridled passion for the fortune of money, and thus enjoy the glory of social, political and economic power to the fullest.

The Portuguese had no ennobling ideals, intellectual values, or interest in culture or the arts. He had only shrewd ideas, and money and economic strength represented the only means for attaining social greatness and earthly happiness, since he had never given any time to matters of a spiritual and eternal nature... He was not interested in the question of life after death, or of the inner victories of the spiritual being as it ascended toward God. His was the conventional God of the doctrines of the past, doctrines incapable of making better individuals or beckoning them with Immortality, but offering paradoxical future destinies involving absurd punishments and rewards devoid of meaning.

On that same day, Manolo summoned Mayuso to a private meeting after work, when they could be alone, and explained to the prospective murderer what had passed through his mind.

He would attract his sordid foe to the office at night. Everything indicated that he would not be accompanied by his bodyguards, but even if he were, the pair would conduct their business. Manolo would take possession of the promissory notes and hand over the necklace and earrings, crowning the event with a carefully prepared drink containing a slow-acting diluted but powerful sedative. They would say goodbye and leave happy or at least looking happy. He, himself, would go home, and the final part would be up to Mayuso, who by this time will have gotten into the Portuguese's car, hiding in the backseat, if the Portuguese had come alone...

He paused, enjoying the hoped-for results beforehand.

He went on:

"I will follow him at a steady distance, and will be ready to help if you need me to. But be careful with the case containing the necklace and earrings. They are a family inheritance and I would never be able to explain their disappearance."

Feeling deeply honored by the opportunity offered to him, poor, ignorant Mayuso thanked his boss, promising to take every precaution possible for the plan not to fail.

They shook hands – an unusual gesture between employer and employee, but common among criminals – and headed for their respective homes, mulling over future events.

On the appointed evening after the foundry had shut down, Manolo remained in his office along with his accomplice. It was springtime and the days were slowly growing warmer as summer approached. The sun still left spots of light among the clouds in the west, while the prognosis of the tragedy hovered in the air.

As if appointed by fate, the Portuguese, relying on his own cunning and the verbal power of seduction that he believed he possessed, dismissed his bodyguards, since after the business with Manolo, he planned to take the jewels to his mistress's house, where he would keep them until he transferred them to his safe deposit box at bank X.

Taking the folder containing the promissory notes, and without having told anyone about the business deal, he leapt with joy just before entering Manolo's office, where he was received jovially by the no less shrewd villain.

They talked about banalities before getting down to the business at hand.

The loan shark presented the documents representing a debt of more than $180,000, a veritable fortune. He had appraised the diamonds at $120,000, so Manolo would still owe an amount that corresponded to a third of the total value of the loan, which could be paid off at the earliest opportunity, along with the corresponding interest.

Instead, Manolo offered just $20,000 to pay off the difference right then and there, and the transaction was completed between smiles and expectations, concealing the criminal abilities of both parties, each wishing to harm the other, as it happens between dishonest people.

Manolo handed over the money and the navy blue velvet case with the jewels. The Portuguese opened the elegant box and could not hide the impact provoked by the glittering stones. Manolo was struck with a strange foreboding, but he could not hide the fascination that dominated him.

The Portuguese put the diamonds in his valise, which was stuffed with other promissory notes. The two shook hands, and, when the creditor was about to leave, the Spaniard proposed that they crown the deal with a glass of good Port wine, naturally preferred by the Portuguese.

Manolo poured the heady liquor into two glasses of precious crystal on a delicate silver tray. The bouquet was quickly captured by the pituitary, producing ineffable pleasure.

After a toast to the celebrated act, the moneylender drank the precious nectar from the grape to the last drop, while his companion skillfully exchanged his own glass for another, which was discreetly hid behind the bottle and which had not been laced with the sedative.

They said goodbye. The Spaniard locked the office, and they left in opposite directions.

Meanwhile, Mayuso had hidden himself in the back seat of the Portuguese's car. The loan shark climbed in, beginning to feel dizzy. He started the car and headed toward the outskirts of the city, where his mistress lived. The toxin quickly took effect, and he stopped the car in a futile attempt to recover. Traffic in the area was very light and there was no one to offer him help.

Realizing that the moment had arrived, Mayuso began strangling him with a nylon cord. Dazed by the sedative, the victim could do nothing and died quickly after a few loud gasps, during which his head fell backward, with his mouth terribly open and his tongue hanging out in desperation for more air. The criminal, deft as a cat, took the valise, opened the car door and fled, soon to be picked up by his boss.

They immediately headed back to the office, where Manolo took the diamonds and the money out of the voluminous briefcase. He wiped it very carefully to remove any traces of fingerprints, then wrapped it in a plastic bag and told Mayuso to bury it somewhere in the brush far from the city.

Manolo poured the remainder of Port wine down the bathroom sink, washed it with a strong detergent, and then carefully wiped off the bottle. He was careful to keep it in order to throw it on some heap of rubbish on the city's outskirts, destroying what might be evidence of the crime, although that particular sedative was widely used throughout much of the world to facilitate such heinous crimes.

Before bidding farewell to his accomplice, he advised him:

"We need to go about our business as if nothing happened in order not to attract attention. Silence will be our best weapon of defense. Since there were no witnesses, it will be almost impossible for the police to find out who committed the murder."

When the moneylender's body was found the next day, the city was in an uproar. The authorities immediately performed an autopsy, noting the strangulation, but also the presence of the narcotic substance in the viscera – evidence of a premeditated crime. The Portuguese's money exchange kept its doors closed and the widow was asked to give some information to the police. Since the briefcase and documents were missing, they were convinced it was a robbery-homicide and they were interested in identifying the probable murderer or who ordered the robbery.

When asked if her husband might have had any enemies, the widow, Gumercinda, was very frank:

"Who doesn't have enemies everywhere nowadays? In addition, my husband was responsible for countless business deals with compatriots, involving securities and documents, sending gold coins abroad and making other cash transactions" – she avoided pronouncing the word "loan sharking," more appropriate and better known by all.

"By chance," the officer asked, "did he have a quarrel with any dissatisfied client, or was he involved in any litigation with a competitor who might want revenge?"

She quickly replied:

"I knew about many of the debtors of our company, but not others, especially since he always feared being a victim of some crime. He preferred to keep me uninformed so that I would not run the same risk. I was always the one responsible for sending money to Portugal, but he did everything else by himself."

She paused, trying to hold back the tears and reducing the emotion of pain, and then proceeded:

"My husband was a very discreet man, and that was one of the reasons for the success of his business. But he did know how to speak at the right time." She wanted to say that he knew how to extort from his victims the money they owed him, under threat of blackmail or something else, which corresponded to being a person endowed with much cruelty, and therefore possessing enemies by the handful.

"Do you have any idea who might have killed him, or ordered it done?"

"No idea," she said, through tears of piercing pain. "But if I do remember anything that might shed light on the crime, I'll let you know."

Dismissed from the interrogation, Gumercinda went home to mourn her dead husband and make arrangements for the funeral and burial, as well as all that was necessary to continue with her life.

The unfortunate news, on the other hand, was a pleasant surprise for many of the infamous businessman's clients, who thought they were free from having to pay their debts to the immoral vulture, making themselves no better than he was.

These shrewd debtors were unaware of the fact that the Portuguese was very well organized and had left behind signed documents as evidence of their commitment. As a result, the no less unscrupulous widow would demand payment later, under penalty of their being reported to the authorities or suffering other unforeseeable consequences.

Manolo, however, was out of the dangerous relationship, due to having asked the creditor for the promissory notes, which he incinerated one by one the very next day.

There was, therefore, a certain amount of panic amongst the unfortunate clientele of the old crow, who had been barbarously sent to the World of Reality.

Doubts and questions multiplied around the tragedy, which relieved some enemies, and worried others no less adverse in potential.

Soon after the shock, Gumercinda and the two minions who used to assist the nefarious dealer asked each other why he had left without his usual protection. After some reflection and discussion of the reasons, they came to the conclusion that he must have gone to meet someone he could trust or someone with whom he was associated. Now, the two bodyguards knew about his extramarital relationship, but they did not tell the widow, because they wanted to keep their job. They liked it and were well compensated for their fidelity. If they told her about the affair now, it could result in her displeasure, and she would feel not only betrayed by her husband but also by his employees. Thus they promised each other not to say anything.

But they themselves sought an explanation for the terrible murder and the circumstances in which it had occurred, not far from the center of the city, where such incidents were unusual.

Stung by curiosity, by the interest in assisting the authorities' investigation of the murder, and by the positive results that could stem from it, they promised to observe and follow any number of suspects who, of course, would surface eventually. They were almost completely unaware of Manolo's involvement with their boss, the large amount of money he owed, or the argument they had had weeks earlier.

At the funeral home where the Portuguese's body was being viewed, many friends, certainly his debtors and employees, as well as respectable people, came to mourn and pay homage, as occurs in such situations.

The comments were the most varied, from those who celebrated him as a real success, considering the struggles he had waged until he arrived at the enviable situation he enjoyed, to others who were more reticent about the origin of his wealth, to his enemies, who gnawed away at his memory with unfortunate epithets and sullen considerations.

"We shall see," said some in the last group, "how this evil and perverse exploiter of many lives will stand before God."

While others replied in kind:

"There's plenty of room in hell for loan sharks and exploiters. That shameful profession has always been condemned. Fortunately, I resorted to his aid only once" – something which was not really true – "because I considered its illegality and the almost complete impossibility of freeing myself because of the extortionate interest."

Someone else added:

"Who would have shortened his wretched life? It doesn't look like a crime committed by the *Blacks*" – the word was saturated with sarcasm and prejudiced disdain – "because no traces were found that could implicate them. It looks to me like something done by very clever people, with the ability to appear to be innocent."

The tone of the comments was almost always the same. Not one person remembered to emit a salutary thought wave, a prayer. Although they claimed to be Christians, all of them lived materialism in its most bestial expression, which is that of sordid interests, of primitive passions.

Among those who went to offer their condolences to the widow and to carry out their social duty to the deceased, were Doctor and Mrs. Albuquerque, their son Júlio, Eneida and Manolo. The first four were sincerely honest; the fifth put on a good show of pretense.

The environment exuded hypocrisy and malaise. People came and went as if they were attending an unpleasant, but unavoidable event. However, due to their religious conviction, which was other than the predominant standard, and to their belief in immortality of the spirit and its communication, the Albuquerques greeted the widow and then concentrated, enveloping the discarnate in vibrations of compassion and peace in order that he might be freed from the bonds of matter, whose effects continue even after the body is buried or cremated. The Portuguese, because of the habits and traditional culture, was to be buried in the local cemetery, which happened that very day with a large number of attendees.

7

MEANINGFUL TRANSFORMATIONS FOR THE GOOD AND FOR SUFFERING

A month after the Portuguese was robbed, the authorities were still right where they were on the first day, with no clue that might help solve the crime. There were several false leads that led nowhere, and the case was among those that were thought to have been perpetrated either by a group of drug addicts or just a solitary assailant. Hence the case was kept open, waiting for a more promising lead.

Manolo and Mayuso went out of their way to avoid each other and acted as they always had, so as not to arouse suspicion.

Manolo, however, began to communicate more spontaneously with his family, now that he felt free of the debt and had gotten his revenge on the enemy who used to threaten him. Moreover, he did not show any sense of remorse or such sentiment.

He became more cheerful toward Eneida and cut back on the alcohol, although he did not give it up altogether. He also began visiting his parents and the Albuquerques, much to everyone's delight, because it gave them more quality time with Esperanza and her parents. There seemed to be no more worries, foretelling a blessed future.

One day, the Boss asked Mayuso to stay at the end of the workday so they could talk; they had not yet addressed the subject of the crime.

Mayuso remained late, as was usual, after everyone else had left, and went to his boss's office, where he was waiting for him with a broad smile of happiness. After being greeted and asked to sit down, Mayuso was told the reason for the meeting.

Manolo got straight to the point:

"In accordance with our plan, it won't be long before we will need to take care of a few of the unattended details."

He paused briefly and then continued:

"It's not a good idea for you to remain in this city. I think it would be best for you to move somewhere else pretty soon, someplace where you can start a new life, support your family, and take care of yourself in other circumstances."

He paused again and continued:

"I'll never be able to repay you as you deserve for the favor you did for me… or for that wretch's many other victims, for that matter. He won't be afflicting so many lives and troubling the people who fell into his web of evil anymore. I've been thinking about your future – yours, your wife's, your little girl's, and your other kids'. You're a strong man, able, hardworking and completely trustworthy. So you deserve a break, and I can give you one. I have some money set aside that will enable you to buy a home to live in and to start a small business – if that's what suits you – or whatever you find most agreeable."

When he heard these words, Mayuso excused himself for interrupting and responded:

"What I did, sir, was no more than my duty, the duty of gratitude for your help in saving my daughter."

"I know that," replied Manolo, touched. "I know your only interest was in helping me. Even so I want to repay you with this favor. It's of utmost importance for my life. So, is there a different city you'd like to move to?

Stunned by the offer, the employee responded:

"Well, my wife and I are from KwaZulu-Natal Province. That's where our roots are. Our closest relatives came from there, like us, looking for a better life..."

"That's even better," Manolo interrupted, "because if you go back there with a bit of financial freedom, you won't arouse any curiosity among your family members... or any envy that might incite them to try to find out where the money came from. I'm really excited about his! So I think that in a few more weeks... a month and a half, or two, we can close this chapter of our lives. Just as a precaution, tell some coworker that, when the time is right, you're thinking about going back to Natal for your wife and daughter's health... In the meantime we can talk about it whenever we need to.

"Oh!" he adduced shrewdly, "And your wife doesn't need to know where the money came from or the details about the move. When the time comes, you'll find a way to explain it... Women talk a lot and they like to brag to their friends, and that would mess up our plan, because just one detail, one little oversight might arouse curiosity and lead to the discovery of our pact."

The two smiled, feeling happy. They shook hands and Mayuso left, almost out of his mind with excitement. He had never thought he would reap fruits with such flavor...

When he arrived home, he told his wife that he wanted to move out of town as soon as he could, stating that he intended to get a loan from his boss, who had been so kind – like when their little girl had gotten ill – so that he could change his life and find personal fulfillment.

His wife had little concern about financial matters. She was devoted to her home, although she did work for a family who entrusted their house to her twice a week for cleaning, which helped with her family's expenses. She was joyful and hopeful about returning to her native Natal, where she hoped to find happiness. Her husband was the one who decided about issues involving the family clan.

Thanks to his change – at least temporary – of behavior, Manolo and his family began to visit the Albuquerque residence more often. On those occasions he had the opportunity to take part in the study of the Gospel in the home. On one such occasion, Evangelina, in trance, acted as an instrument of psychophonic communication by the respected spirit Monsignor Alves da Cunha.

Though psychologically antagonistic to this type of activity, which resulted from spiritualistic convictions adopted by his father-in-law and family members, he could not help but accept the cultural and illuminating encounter.

After the visibly emotional medium offered a compassion-filled prayer to God, Júlio opened *The Gospel according to Spiritism* by Allan Kardec, and choosing a page at random – guided by the family group's spirit mentors – he read the text *True Misfortune,* inserted in chapter V, item 24, dictated by the unforgettable spirit Delfina de Girardin.

As Júlio read the page in a proper and expressive manner, Manolo was struck by the references to true misfortune, the kind that causes moral damage to the soul, whose perverse acts it will have to expunge in pain-filled, liberating reincarnations, when the tears that well up in the heart rise to one's face and pour forth in a continuous suffocating flow, demanding reparation for past wrongs. He could not escape from the two tragic scenes he had caused, which seemed to have been asleep in his unconscious, but which now returned, reinvigorated, as if triggered by a magical process. The young man had to make a great effort not to be affected by a sudden vertigo. Nibbling on his lower lip, a characteristic sign of his angry temperament, he tried hard to control himself. No one noticed his conflict, because they were all focused on the always current and enriching content of the message, especially with regard to the understanding of human occurrences, which are always to be interpreted according to the servile interests of the ego and its derivatives...

Henrique then began formulating philosophical, sociological, ethical, moral, humanitarian and religious considerations, explaining that, actually, misfortune is often a blessing from God that enables wrongdoers to reform themselves with regard to the Cosmic Laws by redeeming the serious crimes that weigh on their spiritual economy. However, success by unlawful means, victory that is based on the unhappiness of others, pretense resulting from heinousness and crime, and victory by suffocating helpless victims – these are what can be considered as true misfortune.

"Society," he explained wisely, "suffers from the atrophy of the sentiments of love and dignity, and believes that winners must not be held back by any situations or persons that appear as an obstacle. They must be bold enough to transcend them, even if it requires uncontrolled violence. That is why the burden of physical, economic, social, psychological and moral suffering weighs on men and women individually, as well as on society in general. It is like a dagger that pierces to the heart of their being, trying to awaken them to a different reality, but which they refuse to accept."

There was an unusual vibration of peace, and a mirific light permeated the dimly lit room.

Manolo was experiencing conflicting sentiments for the first time. In spite of the undeniable emotion of harmony filling his whole body, almost numbing it, he could not master the conflict drawn from his memory, especially that which had culminated in the atrocious murder of the moneylender.

Inspired and wise, Dr. Albuquerque continued his commentary:

"Only when individuals awaken their own consciousness to the understanding of their reality as immortal beings, whose evolution cannot be stopped, will misfortunes and tragedies disappear from the earth, because, according to their acts, they will face the consequences. By understanding the true aims of existence, which go beyond the accumulation of things, even those to which they attach significant value, they will perceive that the attainment of inner peace, the expansion of the sentiment of love, and the accomplishment of endeavors that advance them and society are what will put them on the pathway of happiness. As long as they agonize over power and desire, they will go on feeling dissatisfied, losing themselves in the abyss of disturbing illusions, with goals that are ephemeral in duration and shallow in meaning and content, for in no way do these provide the happiness they long for. It is too enthusiastically said that happiness comes from fulfilling ambitions and experiencing the passions, but that only impels the multitudes along in the shameful and delusional competition for possession, the fulfilment of lust, and greed.

"Human beings are destined for spiritual greatness, the Kingdom of Heaven, to which Jesus referred, but which is only gradually installed in the consciousness and in the heart. All earthly possessions have the value that we attribute to them, and however significant they may be, when loneliness, longing or anguish settle in our hearts, such things are incapable of diminishing it. On the other hand, moral and spiritual acquisitions, such as peace of mind, arising from a responsible conscience resulting from wholesome thoughts, just words and right conduct, inner enrichment through the knowledge and practice of the good, and fraternal service involving compassion and help, increase the sentiments of love, charity and inner enlightenment. Of course, the struggle for the honest acquisition of food, clothing, shelter, and a dignified, responsible social position are human goals that must be worked out, but on a secondary level, arising from having chosen the transcendent acquisitions first.

"True and misperceived misfortunes have these characteristics: the first type of misfortunes are when individuals forget about or disregard duties that extol and harmonize, whereas the latter involve experiences that offer the treasures of renewal and inner growth through deep reflections in the bed of suffering, through trials involving loved ones, and through the incessant struggle to meet one's needs."

When he finished after having offered broader considerations, one could see that a wave of peace had invaded the room, rendering it a resplendent sanctuary of immaterial beauties, where spiritual zephyrs moved about, entrusted with protecting and sustaining the ideals of the human creature.

Despite being troubled due to some of Henrique's thoughts having wounded him directly, Manolo, too, experienced the same tranquility that hovered over the small group gathered there.

Then, during a natural pause, Evangelina began to speak mediumistically in a melodious and slow voice, expressing a personality very different from her own.

It was the study group's mentor, Monsignor Alves da Cunha, who had come to add more insight into Madame de Girardin's message in *The Gospel according to Spiritism*.

After a fraternal greeting and a few words of encouragement to his incarnate friends, he began:

"The world hides true misfortune in the folds of its cloak of ignorance, thus it either goes unnoticed or is sometimes admired. On the other hand, the world places excessive value on occurrences, which are actually invitations to profound thought and inner balance, but which it labels as afflictions or misfortunes because they are clothed in momentary unpleasantness due to the fact that they expose the individual to suffering, trials and faith.

"One could argue that those who are going through transitory afflictions are actually blessed because they are being burnished for future experiences. They are redeeming 'promissory notes' in preparation for inexpressible existential and spiritual joys. Hence, it is not the anxious, suffering or misunderstood who are to be considered misfortunate, but those who oppress them with their meanness, who despise them, who hinder their ascension, who steal from them and exhaust them with unjust and cruel labor. Those who act in this way are preparing shackles for themselves that will imprison them in the future for having brought affliction on others in the present. The victims of such afflictions are actually free, whereas those who inflict the despair are morally imprisoned in the invisible jail cells of future remorse, the antechamber of bitter trials and expiations.

"All those who resignedly suffer the heinousness of apartheid acquire the virtues of patience and love, of overcoming the noxious, primitive tendencies that dominate the inner landscape of their character, the perverse inclinations that still remain of their former state of moral primitivism. Nevertheless, this does not rule out nonviolent struggle for the elimination of this social scourge, which still keeps humanity perverse and backward. Hence, those men and women who think they are superior because of their skin color, their race, the momentary capricious situation of their fate, which has made them rich and powerful, are miserable creatures because they keep themselves morally poor and spiritually backward. And this also applies to all those who misappropriate – often criminally – property that does not belong to them, or who have lost property because of bad business deals, unsecured loans, committing heinous deeds, which they cunningly conceal, but which they cannot annul in their conscience nor hide from the Sovereign Laws of Life."

There was a timely interregnum, while Manolo, directly hit, felt a dart pierce his conscience. But instead of pondering the spirit mentor's guidance, he became agitated, wondering if this "offense" was directed at him, for he viewed the admonition as a personal insult. Nevertheless, he angrily dismissed what he was hearing, believing it to be an unfortunate coincidence of content, or a platitude that Evangelina was using to keep the family under control.

Since he did not have a profound vision of reality, nor did he practice even superficial meditation, he did not have the mental resources to heed the timely warning and call-to-reason in order to rehabilitate himself while he was experiencing the blessed occasion.

He wondered how it was possible that the relatively uneducated Evangelina could produce an inarguably impressive spectacle of such magnitude.

He had not yet finished his negative thinking, gripped by the conflict of suspicion and the barbs of truth, when the spirit continued:

"Whenever individuals are surprised by the truth during their evolution toward God, they dwell on absurd sophisms or explanations in order to maintain their usual comfort or their complicity with crime and vulgarity, which generally predominate in the behavior of all individuals. Life, however, surprises all of us through the vehicle of death, which beckons us to the other dimension of thought and life, when our consciousness, free of cerebral impositions, awakens *in totum* to the understanding of who we are. Therefore, blessed are those who, faced with the truth, do not turn to escape mechanisms or palliative formulations, by which they would avoid confronting their responsibilities as they work out their rehabilitation. None, however, can escape themselves. It is not necessary to account to others for their acts, whether noble or awful, for the problem is internal, personal, non-transferable. And thanks to this two-fold conduct – *the inner, which is authentic, and the outer, which presents itself as conventional, that of appearance* – countless individuals cave in to the neurotic disorders of depression or severe psychoses, precisely because they want to avoid reflecting on the monstrous acts that flow from their real character."

"Well, that's just too much!" thought Manolo. "What kind of nonsense is this? Was this some devil who had come to reproach him for his conduct? How could what was being said be an exact and direct response to his very thoughts?"

Stunned, taken by a deathly, trembling pallor, he wanted to stand up, but he thought it might arouse some suspicion among those who were listening contritely to what Evangelina was saying – or was it really a spirit after all?

The noble guide continued his illustrative elucidation:

"It is always easy to come up with a lie to deny what is right and correct, because it enables one to give continuity and vitality to one's foolishness and disturbing commitments. God, however, who is all Love, does not cease to guide those who stray from the good way of right conduct, so that when invited to their inevitable redemption, to the recomposition of order, they do not believe they have been victims of circumstances, or claim ignorance and lack of proper guidance for conduct. The essential thing is not the punishment of criminals, but their rehabilitation, and the whole endeavor must be aimed at the wrong, the condemnable act, giving way to order, to social balance, to the dignifying of the human being.

"We have all traveled difficult paths; we have experienced reprehensible behavior, and today, in the spirit world, those of us who have overcome the most painful situations must strive to awaken others so that they do not suffer the same regrettable misunderstandings that we did, even after we have recovered from their disastrous consequences. Therefore, we dare not judge any conduct, however improper it may be. Our sole purpose is to provide guidance to hasten the coming of the *Kingdom of God* to the earth's physical inhabitants, preventing them from falling into real disasters."

He paused again for a while, then returned to happy comments, and after addressing words of encouragement and moral comfort to all, he said goodbye, leaving gentle vibrations of happiness, which were felt by all except Manolo.

After the meeting with the spirit ended with a prayer anointed with love and thanksgiving, light comments were offered by the happy family, although Manolo did not participate, and then a tasty snack was served to all.

Manolo, however, disguising the eruption of more-severe conflicts, tried to understand what had just happened, but it would have been much easier if he had simply accepted the reality of the facts, without wasting time on misguided and absurd self-explanations. From the initial theme, drawn *at random* for discussion, to the comments made by Dr. Albuquerque and the spirit messenger, all had been directed at him as divine inspiration to keep him from proceeding with the future steps that he had already outlined in his perverse mind. Nonetheless, stubbornness, that child of ignorance and pride, blocked his discernment, preventing him from making broader and happier flights concerning exemplary conduct. Sadly, educated according to the conventional moneymaking standards that emigres set for themselves while outside their home country in order to return to it later with a fortune – or at least regally well-off – to enjoy a happy life, Manolo and his family members never really connected with the generous country that had opened its welcoming doors to them and their economic independence. After reaching the goal – accumulating a fortune – all that remained was the materialist-hedonistic interest of leaving the soil of prosperity behind to go and enjoy the lands from which they had originated. Thus, there was no mental time for the spiritual refreshment of religious belief, and he remained on the surface of his traditional, uncommitted and formalistic faith, which was more social and external than of enlightening profundity.

True, not all emigrants behave similarly. However, there is, even if unconsciously, that desire to return to the soil where one was born once the trials and sufferings that accompany every process of emigration have passed.

Returning home, rather than introjecting the emotional and fluidic benefits of the meeting, he became introspective, downcast, uneasy, and disgusted with what had happened, which he insisted on denying, even though the facts showed otherwise.

This attitude had not changed when he went to bed, leaving his wife worried about him because she did not understand: she thought that her husband would have benefited greatly from the beautiful explanations that had been offered.

Let us be frank: Manolo was beginning to feel the mental constriction of those whose organic life he had reaped but had not annihilated. They were slowly attuning to his mental power plant in an attempt to install psychic outlets for obsessing him in the future.

In that state of mind, dominated by headless rebelliousness, without having benefited from the lenitive of prayer before physical repose, he was soon overcome by sleep. He felt himself leave his body, and he *dreamed* that the Portuguese, with the terrible look in which he had died, suffocated and deformed by suffering, rose fearsomely and shouted at him with clenched hands, as if desiring to strangle him:

"What did you do to me? I trusted in your dishonor, but you murdered me like a coward! Bear in mind that you shall not escape me. I will follow you into hell or I will lead you into it, charging you with the infamy, the crime, the debt you stole from me."

Sweating profusely and shaking with dread in the throes of agony, awakening Eneida, he tried to justify himself:

"That crime was not my idea!"

"Oh, you don't think I know, you wicked coward and accuser? ... I know it was your servant. I'll make him pay too when the time comes... But you're the one who's responsible. You're the one who wanted me dead. You just didn't know how to go about it. That pariah just suggested the best way. You were the one who laced my drink with drugs to make it easier to strangle me. Do you have any idea of what I've suffered and what I've been going through? I'm as crazed as you are. I'll never leave you alone till human or divine justice catches up with you. You'll never have a night of peace, of rest again because I'll be waiting for you on this side of life, watching like a hungry cheetah. You don't believe in the True Life. I didn't either until I came here, dying without dying, yearning for annihilation that never came. No, I awoke to pay for all my wrongs, all the illegal things I did, all my cruelties toward my debtors... I'm also suffering the scourge of other enemies who had been waiting for me, and the regret for the evil that I practiced to get the gold and money that stayed behind on the earth... The diamond necklace you stole from me will also be your ruin ... Now, wake up, you bastard!"

With a deafening scream, and after babbling unintelligible words to the concerned Eneida, Manolo, struggling angrily, woke up in a panic.

He was shaking like a leaf and sweating all over. Realizing he was back in the objective world, he brought his hand to his chest in a reflexive motion of calming his dysrhythmic heart, and exclaimed:

"Oh, thank God! What a horrible nightmare! I knew that Spiritism business would do me harm. That's why I hate things condemned by the Church. There's good reason for it."

Surprised, his wife reprimanded him:

"I don't get your aversion to Spiritism. You don't know a thing about it ... Good cannot do harm. The wonderful things we heard couldn't have upset you – unless they reached some hidden corner in your conscience, causing you to react."

"What have you heard?" he interrupted violently, upset, aggressive. "What did your mother tell you about me? As a fortuneteller and demoniac, she has to know about what hasn't even happened yet in order to dupe idiots, using the magic arts to impress and control. That's not going to happen to me. I'll be on the lookout against her spells and the accusations of her spirits."

Eneida was shocked by what she had just heard, and shot back:

"You may be my husband, but I will not allow you to make such accusations against my mother. Her life of honor and sacrifice is beyond suspicion. She's not a demoniac or a fortuneteller; she's an extraordinary medium and can communicate with the spirit world and its inhabitants, especially those of a high order, the ones who come to visit us to give us good counsel. I don't understand what has happened or is happening to you, but I'll not keep still against absurd accusations like those."

"Be that as it may," he said arrogantly, "don't invite me to any more practices of witchcraft like tonight's ... And your upstanding mother doesn't need to come to our house again to pollute my daughter with her evil practices ... And that's all I'm going to say on the matter."

"Fine, I'll speak to her; she'll just miss her own daughter and granddaughter for sure because, for you, there is no other feeling than that of compassion and mercy, in your pride and pettiness."

Hurt, the young wife got up and went to sleep in the bedroom of Esperanza, who was in the sweet lap of child's sleep, journeying along beaches of light in the Region whence she came.

The criminal, completely devoid of spiritual assets and moral resources, also got up and went in search of the whiskey, as do all those who have lost their way and proceed without a roadmap of security or peace.

This was a special night, the start of torments that would never end for Manolo.

In his hut, that same night, Mayuso was beset with an almost identical *dream*.

Feeling happy about returning to his province of Natal, as his boss had promised days before, he had filled his mind, during that time, with plans that he would make a reality later, when he arrived back in his native city. He imagined how he would hide the money, spending it slowly so as not to attract attention. It would seem to some that his life in Vanderbijlpark had enabled him to save up enough for a less painful return. Others would think that his boss had rewarded him for special services rendered, and of course he would not disclose what they had been. After a while, everyone would get used to his situation, making life less painful.

That same night, however, he experienced for the first time the strange confrontation with the Portuguese, who appeared to him bearing the marks of the strangulation, plus some other deformities that made him a ghastly specter. He shouted in fury at Mayuso:

"You bastard, why did you murder me?" What did I ever do to you? Did you have to become a heartless hit man just to please your Boss? Do you think that you'll escape your crime just because he's going to reward you with money? That money will be cursed because it's mine, and it's going to bring you a lot of misery. Don't kid yourself – you'll never be able to hide from me. I'll be the shadow of your conscience and I'll never leave you alone. From hell, where you sent me, I'll follow you, like a ruthless devil, until I have sucked the blood and the sweat off your face and body to the last drop."

Shaking in despair on his miserable bed and groaning painfully, he woke up suddenly to his frightened wife, who had heard some of what he had said during the nightmare.

"It seems that a demon took the form of an unknown creature and came to scare me to death," he justified himself as he regained his lucidity. "This has never happened to me before. God have mercy."

He got up, feeling the presence of a guilty conscience for the first time. He did not get back to sleep and stayed awake until he went to work very early, as was his habit.

As soon as the day dawned and the city began to stir, Manolo, too, headed for the factory without saying goodbye to his wife, who was still asleep in Esperanza's room.

Coincidentally, the two accomplices arrived at the same time and met each other at the entrance.

Mayuso noticed the pallor and the dark circles under his boss's eyes, and asked him, respectfully, *en passant:*

"Is the Boss not feeling so good?"

Grumpy and sincere, the Spaniard answered, still numb from sleep and alcohol:

"The Devil visited me last night, so no, I'm not feeling so good, actually."

"What do you mean?" Mayuso asked, concerned.

"I had an awful nightmare involving someone who's dead..."

Mayuso did not let him finish the sentence:

"Me too. I swear to my Boss that that dead man returned bearing the marks of his death and he threatened me with cruel vengeance. I was so terrified that I woke up in despair and couldn't get back to sleep. If it happens again, I'm going to look up our tribe's sorcerer and ask him for protection."

"And you believe that will work? Well, if it does, let me know and I'll go too." And he laughed loudly, the symptom of a psychotic disorder and mockery.

Both accomplices headed for their posts, totally impressed by the *coincidence* of nightmares.

Instead of considering the legitimacy of the spirit phenomenon, bearing in mind that his discarnate victim was able to return to the terrestrial proscenium because he had survived death, Manolo became even more fixated on the idea that perhaps his mother-in-law was behind the events, causing this trouble, which she had obviously conjured up using demonic influence for some purpose which he could not identify at the moment, but which he would discover later. Consequently, his animosity toward the worthy woman increased.

That was a tumultuous day for both of the accomplices of the tragedy that had been imposed on the inclement exploiter.

The association of characters in the same drama of fate was following the Law of Cause and Effect, which no one can escape in the course of evolution. Sovereign, it rules lives as it accompanies individuals while they follow the path toward their perfection, which, at first, is achieved through painful effort as they free themselves from the crudeness of the instincts, advancing through reason, and then attaining intuition, before finally pursuing the state of angelhood...

8
THE SINISTER SHADOW FOLLOWING THE MURDERER

Six months after the cowardly crime against the Portuguese, the police investigations had gone nowhere. There was not a single one clue that might lead to the discovery of its agents or instigators.

As he had agreed with Manolo, Mayuso created an atmosphere of trust among his colleagues, telling them of his desire to return to his place of origin. It seemed that the local climate was not auspicious for the little girl, who had fallen ill again with respiratory problems. It was a perfectly understandable excuse, the same he had given to his wife, who was completely ignorant of the entire plot by the odious conspirators.

His boss had been generous, as he had promised, providing him with gold coins, which he could exchange for money at an appreciated rate, as well as an amount in currency, which would guarantee him a standard of living entailing a life without the heavy work to which he had always devoted himself.

Consequently, he was able to transfer his residency quietly without the appearance of trying to escape from something. The move to the province had no repercussions in the wretched neighborhood, having sold his hovel for a trifle, which would tie him over until he could find the job that suited him best.

Meanwhile, the Spaniard felt safer and well-compensated for his audacity, having freed himself from the ruthless loan shark he had hated for so long.

Concurrently, as if experiencing a neurotic compulsion, he began to feel increasingly attracted to and enraptured by the diamonds. Their penetrating glitter and cold composition fascinated him. He was so fascinated, in fact, that he transferred the necklace and earrings to the safe at his place of business, where he would look at them frequently after being careful to lock the office door.

"Could it really be true," he would often ask himself, "that, as a rule, diamonds are bearers of an ill-fated destiny for their owners?"

Indeed, there was a certain consistency in many of such claims, involving splendid diamond-studded crowns sported by powerful monarchs, motivating envy and passion and resulting in heinous crimes. In a way, his, too, were ill-fated diamonds because they were responsible for two barbarous deaths, and were magnetically stained with blood.

As he pondered the almost magical attraction the stones had on his sick personality, he could not stifle his enthusiasm. He laughed and almost shouted out loud:

"Ill-fated or not, they're mine, whether or not Eneida wears them. They belong to me, and I shall defend them with my very life if I have to."

We can state that Manolo was displaying stronger signs of alienation, which was spilling over into his attitudes and mental behavior.

Little by little he was becoming more miserly, distrustful, and stubborn. And, in his diseased narcissism, whenever he would make a decision, he considered himself better than others, especially the relatives on both sides of the family – his and his wife's. As a consequence, his relationship with Eneida began to deteriorate, but because of Esperanza, it was not degenerating into an unfortunate process of immediate separation. The little one was becoming increasingly beautiful and more loving toward her tormented father, who, at her side, felt renewed, calm, more docile and sympathetic.

No doubt, the girl embodied purity and tenderness, which touched her father in particular since she was actually a beloved spirit who had returned to assist him during his difficult, evolutionary ascent. Regrettably, although he had received the best resources possible from the Divinity for a happy existence, marked by moral achievements and spiritual progress, he had compromised himself. He had backslid into crime due to moral inheritances that weighed on his evolutionary economy as a consequence of the nefarious life he had lived before in that region of South Africa, when he had yielded to greed and moral missteps, which still tainted his character, making him rebellious.

The Rodríguez family was tired and had returned to Palma de Mallorca, where they hoped to finish up their earthly existence. After they had accumulated large financial resources, most of which they had managed to transfer to Spain, they decided to hand over the business to their children. Sooner or later it would belong to them, and all agreed that

Manolo would be in charge of managing it. On the other hand, Piedad, the married daughter, who also enjoyed financial independence – because of her husband, also an Iberian, and a high ranking official in one of the local banks – had no interest in getting involved with the business. Jaime, the other son, was a playboy and was not interested in the business either. He preferred to receive a monthly allowance and was always asking for a raise in order to finance his whims.

Consequently, Manolo had become the real manager and administrator of the company, which specialized in iron, steel and other metal moldings for the construction of grids, wire netting, fences and special equipment for residences and business. Although the country was going through difficult times, this industrial branch had become quite profitable, particularly because large companies, especially those working with construction, had decided to outsource their activity.

Meanwhile, the young administrator's nights were sheer terror. The *spirit shadows* of the enemies who had suffered his ire did not allow him to rest. They threatened him, terrified him with a truanesque and ferocious appearance, informing him that it would all just be a matter of time.

He would wake up screaming, bathed in sweat, wild-eyed, his heart in dysrhythmia, and feeling as if death were imminent...

Eneida, equally frightened, would try to help him, but he would rebuff her and seek tranquility in a bottle of whiskey, always within reach of his shaking hands.

Ever since the Rodríguez family had moved to the Balearics, Dr. Albuquerque also realized that his was a struggle without great economic benefit. He and his wife dreamed of saving up enough money to return to Portugal, now that the dream of a happy Angola had vanished with the tragedies of the civil war, in which the three political parties were all dissatisfied and incapable of implementing an appropriate administration for the country, each group being more interested in exploiting the mineral riches, bathing the country in rivers of blood. Countless landmines, buried in the generous and promising ground, reaped the lives of children, uninformed natives, and the hateful military personnel, who killed each other without any holding to any ideal or philosophy that promised peace and progress for the people...

The always captivating Doctor Albuquerque had tried countless times to reconcile with Manolo after the episode that had upset him so much when he had fruitlessly studied the Gospel in the Home. Evangelina's mere presence would nearly send him into a rage. It was a crude reaction by his guilty conscience, which strove not to be identified with the dreadful behavior that he had allowed himself and would certainly repeat, due to the lack of ethical values and any other moral commitment toward life.

Thanks to her sensitivity, the capable medium was able to discern the perverse spiritual presences that were tormenting Manolo and she would envelop him as much as possible in vibrations of peace and renewal.

Impervious to lofty sentiments and steadily becoming an alcoholic, he openly avoided get-togethers with his wife's family, causing Eneida to become more and more resentful toward him as the situation became more complicated.

Life, however, has its own laws, which are independent of human passions. They always apply in conformance with the higher determinations, indispensable to the progress and illumination of consciousnesses. Hence, they bend the neck of the most stubborn and perverse, subjecting them to their will and their demands, which no one can escape.

Such was the case regarding the homicide ten months after the now almost completely forgotten crime. Gumercinda, the widow, had received almost immediate consolation by consorting with one of her deceased husband's former bodyguards. Quite happy with this arrangement, she hounded with exploitative fury the victims who fell into her clutches, under the shine of precious metals and the eagerness to take out usurious loans. The police, in turn, more and more accustomed to the tenebrous wave of atrocities, were becoming corrupt, open to bribery, because everything indicated that the revolution promised by the autochthons would actually happen, a revolution that could erupt at any moment without warning.

The venerable black clergyman[8], an elegant orator with indomitable courage, could not bear the suffering of his people, and began to make his voice heard, while the great leader[9], imprisoned unjustly, was forced to remain silent. The former used disregarded human rights and the Gospel to arouse the interest of the great nations that condoned the conditions imposed by the dominant regime.

His voice would soon rise to the heights of international consciences and he would receive the Nobel Peace Prize, making himself heard and sensitizing the world to the superlative pains that were rending the black soul of the former English colony.

Freedom is like an untamed bird, which, bound in shackles of steel, after a thousand attempts to break them, finally does and wings its way toward the infinite, where

---

8   Bishop Desmond Tutu – Spirit author's note
9   Nelson Mandela – Publisher's note.

it soars, proud and happy. No one can hinder freedom indefinitely, because its destiny is to make all the men and women of the world independent, born to be free like the air, the waters that run across the soil, overcoming vast distances until they reach the seas and oceans...

The Rodríguez family was aware of Manolo's pitiful state. They were further informed about it by Eneida, who, although forbidden from visiting her family, would schedule meetings with them whenever possible in commercial establishments, or in restaurants, when, now and then, she would take Esperanza and her governess to see her grandparents and uncle, at the risk of an unpleasant scandal if caught. But because it is unjust, every wrongful prohibition engenders in those who suffer from it the need to get around it, as if they were greedy for air that was becoming scarce...

During one of the weekly meetings, the venerable spirit Alves da Cunha explained that, as a means of purifying him of his rebelliousness, Manolo would be invited to do some serious reflecting, and that the family should continue to envelop him in vibrations of peace and renewal, trusting in God and the future.

The Albuquerque family had worked hard and had been able to save enough money to buy a small business, which would allow them a shorter work schedule. They were just waiting for the transaction to be finalized.

In the meantime, during one of his nocturnal crises, as he was trying to free himself from aggressors who had immobilized him in the spirit realm, Manolo went into convulsions because of his despair. He fell out of bed and dislocated his shoulder, and only realized it when he later regained consciousness, although Eneida, having no other alternative, tried to help him by calling her parents, who rushed over to provide medical support.

Manolo was taken by ambulance to the hospital, where a number of X-rays were taken, some of which revealed the dislocated shoulder, which was reset and then immobilized. An EKG was performed to determine the cause of the seizure, but was unsuccessful.

After he had come out from under the anesthesia, he was informed about the disastrous incident and the measures that had been taken, especially by his in-laws, to alleviate the pain.

Frightened, he had no choice but to confess to Dr. Albuquerque – although without details – the terrible nightmares that had been occurring almost every night during his sleep, exhausting his nerves and strength, and nearly driving him mad.

Dr. Albuquerque listened respectfully. The narrative further confirmed the news by the kindly spirit guide, as well as his prediction of the disturbing incident, because it would surely be repeated with more disastrous effects. There could be no doubt that Manolo was being obsessed.

With great skill, Dr. Albuquerque clarified the fact that the phenomenon of death only frees the imprisoned spirit; it does not annihilate its life. He explained that this is the distinctive thesis of all the world's religious doctrines.

And, taking advantage of Manolo's momentary weakness, he stated kindly:

"Our acts produce vibratory equivalents that make it possible to communicate with those who have put off the clothing of flesh. Depending on the level, there is attunement between higher order spirits and unhappy ones, or, according to the conventional religious language, between angels, saints and demons/obsessors... This occurs quite often during times of the spirit's partial disengagement through physiological sleep. In the history of the lives of saints, artists, poets, martyrs, scientists, and ordinary people, this communication has been constant, and the reports are quite touching regarding both the spiritual glories and the sufferings involved. So, it is not surprising that, in the psychoanalytic study of dreams and their interpretations through symbols, it is possible to identify the causes of the conflicts that afflict human beings. Well, people's actions are recorded in their deep unconscious mind. It is not only those that occur in the present existence, but also those that took place in many previous ones that constitute the process of evolution. These conflicts arise symbolically; others are experienced again, and in this course of events, the spirits with whom we have been involved return and produce either sublime dreams or terrible dreams and nightmares."

While benefitting from the gentle and beneficent radiations by his illustrious father-in-law for the first time, Manolo listened with serenity, in an attempt to understand. The explanations seemed logical to him. With his mind free of the toxic fluids that had dominated him of late, he asked:

"Does that mean that, in my case in particular, these worsening nightmares might be caused by the souls of the dead?"

"Exactly!" the doctor confirmed. "They are spirits who, for one reason or another, do not sympathize with you or have been your victims in some past existence and now wish to avenge themselves for the evils they suffered… The dimension of time is always relative. What we may see as a long period of physical time may be expressed quite differently in another dimension of space. As long as we are subject to the earth's rotation about its axis and its translational movement around the sun, we experience one dimension of time, which

is different on other planets and on the course of the Infinite...
This is how we can understand Eternity, the before and after
of what we call time – always a disturbing question for our
reasoning, which is a slave to temporal and spatial boundaries.

"Remembering Jesus, who returned after three days
in the tomb to prove survival after death, we will be more
comforted by the resurrection phenomenon that is within
reach of all beings…"

"Even the animals?" Manolo interrupted.

"Life is a continuous whole. It does not end in one form
to carry on in another. Rather, it goes from one expression to
another, continuing indefinitely. As we recall Lavoisier's concept
that 'In nature nothing is created, nothing is lost, everything
changes,' we find that it applies not only to physical form, but
to all structures in which life presents itself. The psyche, which
is the primary form with which God creates beings, proceeds
from the molecular agglutinations of minerals to plants, wherein
the first sense stimuli and an embryonic nervous system appear,
unleashing its innate possibilities. It then advances through the
animal kingdom, wherein it develops the instinct to finally reach
the human state, in which intelligence, sentiment, reason, and
consciousness begin to shine in order to advance in the future
to encounter Divinity. Thus, everything dies to be transformed,
disappearing from one structure to appear in another, becoming
subtler and subtler until it becomes light, for we all come from
the Divine Light, the Supreme Focal Point."

The Christian thinker paused briefly in order to let
Manolo absorb the enlightenment, and then continued,
taking advantage of Manolo's state of receptivity:

"Psychic interchange is greater than it might seem in
the world. After all, everything we see and touch is composed

of energy, and it is only natural for there to be a continuous exchange of vibratory movements between all and everything that possesses the same energetic quality. The occurrence of this process of communication is therefore unavoidable, whether it occurs consciously or not, yielding results of various expressions. When we are aware of this potential, we are careful to avoid remaining in the bands of pessimism, of rebelliousness, of moral aberrations, which always facilitate the attracting of equally unhappy, low-order beings. But when we are unaware of it, it is only natural that we become victims of its dictates, which results in pain and affliction."

"And how can we guard against this pernicious influence, if it does exist?"

"Of course it does. We can protect ourselves against it by changing our mental frame of mind: raising the standards of our thoughts, entering other psychic realms, offering prayers anointed with love, submitting to God's will, practicing Christian virtues, especially charity, which is an excellent bond with Divinity. When higher energies are generated by the psyche and absorbed by the psychological organism, as well as by the physiological, these behaviors can be seen as vaccines against the sick and degenerative processes to which we are all subject. This is one of the reasons why we meet at least once a week to pray as a family, generating magnetic defenses against evil and evil individuals…"

There was silence, which seemed natural.

Manolo broke in:

"Ever since my parents moved to Europe, I've been seriously considering changing occupations, because my current one is too exhausting. I also think that my state of mind and spirit is due to stress and setbacks in relation to Jaime, who wants

125

nothing more than to squander money on what pleases him" – he was being hypocritical, for he himself was squandering the family's wealth by dishonest means – "while Piedad is less and less interested in the company. She doesn't need it, even though she enjoys the good results of my exhausting work. Over the past few days, I've been thinking of selling the property and our patent, of seeking another way of life. It's not urgent, because we are financially independent. Since labor is one of the best therapies available to humans, I would like to continue working, providing for my family and planning for the future. I'm still quite young and I have enough time for happiness, which should also extend to my family and those around me."

Dr. Albuquerque was enthusiastically surprised by his son-in-law's decision since it supported his own most-cherished plans. Now he would have a bona fide opportunity to change the course of his life by changing occupations, ceasing to work at night, and living a normal existence.

"I'm pleasantly surprised. If that is really what you want for yourself and your family, I would like to say that, lately, I too have been thinking of changing occupations. Of course, I have managed to secure some financial stability, and so I've been looking for something in my current area of metallurgy to provide for the future. It will be a matter that we could examine later after you've gotten reestablished, when, depending on the possibilities, we can discuss the matter without detriment to either of us, because, through my estate or yours, we will always have our heirs."

A few more details were added, and since Manolo needed rest in order to recover, Dr. Albuquerque excused himself and quietly left the room, which was plunged into darkness as the blinds were lowered to prevent excess light.

If Dr. Albuquerque had been more assertive and had applied bioenergy to the patient, he would have helped him gain an amount of inner peace, even if he was suffering conflict from the ignoble acts he had committed. Such wholesome energy, vitalized by prayer, would have penetrated the organism of the spiritual patient, revitalizing him, dislocating the ruthless obsessor, even if momentarily. However, due to normal scruples not to afflict or irritate Manolo, Dr. Albuquerque had avoided using a prime therapy of great utility.

Manolo entered the *realm of dreams* again and faced his enemies, who reproached him, reaffirming their plan to eliminate him from among incarnates, intent as they were in meting out the justice that human laws had failed to apply.

Terror-stricken and stimulated by his ignorance of the reality of the spirit world, the patient tried to exorcise the spirits, calling them the Devil and Satan, and using traditional and superstitious cabalistic words. Even so, he was ruthlessly attacked by both obsessors, who laughed at him and, almost dragging him along the dark pathways of the lowest erraticity,[10] they finally allowed him to return to his body, more exhausted and frightened than before.

Eneida, who was in the room, witnessing his labored breathing, tried to pray, to plead for divine help since the human assistance seemed ineffective.

Manolo saw her in the semi-darkness and confessed in agony:

"The Devil is after me and is crushing me with the tenacity of his ruthless pursuit. I don't know how long I can take it."

He began weeping profusely in the fever of remorse, which would do his conscience good. If on the one hand

---

10 Erraticity – the interval between reincarnations. – Tr.

such remorse is beneficial in that it relieves the anguish of the guilty, on the other hand it provides a more powerful grip to adversaries because they find resonance of their thoughts in the mental house of the victim, hence establishing the contact and dispute, the arguing and the stormy dialogue that lead to madness, although, as in Manolo's case, not always immediate.

Eneida was truly sympathetic. She approached her husband, which had not happened for quite some time, stroked his cold sweat-soaked head, kissed his pale fear-filled face, and said tenderly:

"Trust in God! No evil can overcome the divine force within us, and which we can draw on when we are linked to the Father of Mercy. This may not be the best time to bring it up, but I've noticed that you've been increasingly turning away from religion, heavenly communion and prayer, which are the treasures we possess to make our lives happy. This unknown thing that has been tormenting you is responsible for your present state. But you can overcome anything if you seek to rebuild your inner world and try to understand that there are other priceless values, which outweigh money and power, enriching those who seek peace."

Her words were impregnated with so much gentleness and love that they found resonance in the beloved patient.

In fact, Eneida was being strongly inspired by her guardian angel, who was interested in the recovery of the marriage, which would happen if Manolo changed his attitude. There is never a lack of resources for rehabilitating any crimes that have been committed. The Lord of Life does not desire the punishment of offenders, but their recovery, their renewal, their return to the path of good.

As he listened to her, Manolo realized how far he was from balance and the joy of living. With his mind divided by conflicts, he felt as if lucidity had abandoned him, for his mind remained fixated on its unconfessable interests. Thus thinking so, he let the tears, now of healthy emotion and of acknowledgement, run gently out of his eyes.

He took his wife's hands and kissed them silently, as if he were committing himself again to the responsibility that he had set aside, or as if he were promising a change of behavior that could no longer be put off.

They talked quietly, without aggression or resentfulness, planning to return to unforgotten days of happiness.

The psychic climate generated by the vibrations of peace and hope engulfed the couple. Manolo had calmed down and fell asleep again, but without having to face his enemies.

Eneida left the room, approached her parents, thanked them for their help, explained that everything was now under control, and reassured them that she could take care of him now.

At the physician's suggestion, she went home, because everything indicated that the night would be one of organic recovery for her husband. He would be under the supervision of a nursing assistant qualified to deal with the situation, which no longer seemed serious.

9
UNEXPECTED EVENTS

After the brief conversation with his ailing son-in-law, Dr. Albuquerque came home even happier than normal and told his wife what had happened. She too was thrilled. "Our prayers have been heard!" she exclaimed.

"What is more, we won't have to worry as much about the business because, in light of the fact that the Rodríguez family has become financially independent by working hard in the metallurgical business, we know it will be prosperous for us too. I believe that if Manolo's desire is authentic, we can invest our savings confidently, with our eyes set on the future."

Sharing in his parents' joy, Júlio asked respectfully:

"What will Manolo do if he does transfer his source of work and income to us or someone else in these difficult days besetting the country?"

"Well," Dr. Albuquerque replied, "he must have something more profitable in mind. But that's none of our concern. We need to remember that Manolo is very ambitious and fearless in everything he does. We only want to reduce the burden of sacrifices that weigh on our own shoulders. Working at night is very demanding and is slowly wearing us out."

"If the matter is to be discussed again," said Evangelina, "further clarification will be needed regarding the company,

its fiscal and economic situation, its debts – everything, really...
We still do not know our son-in-law all that well, and since
he continues to be an instrument of disconcerting attitudes,
it would be well-advised that the procedures for acquiring
the business be handled by competent lawyers, whose job it
will be to avoid legal ... and emotional issues. They won't be
emotionally involved so they will be able to take care of the
details and make demands that would not go over well if we
handled it ourselves."

"Exactly!" replied Henrique. "I had already thought
about that, and I brought it up at the time he mentioned his
plan to sell the company. Since we must avoid financial ruin
a second time, I thought of employing the services of Dr. José
Leal de Almeida. We've known him well and have had a very
good relationship with him ever since the old days in Angola.
I'll meet with him at the earliest opportunity, giving him an
account of what we plan to do and discussing the possibilities
within our reach, so that he can take care of the negotiations
at the earliest opportunity."

And smiling, nibbling his lower lip, as was his habit
when cheerful, he added:

"We know how good Spaniards are when it comes to
business, especially our temperamental son-in-law."

"But they're not very good soldiers, contrary to what
they used to think, because we defeated them in the Battle of
Aljubarrota, and then built the monastery[11] commemorating
our victory."

---

11 The *Monastery of Santa Maria da Vitória* (or *Monastery* of *Batalha*) was
built to commemorate the Portuguese victory in the Battle of Aljubarrota,
fought between the Kingdom of Portugal and the Crown of Castile on
August 14, 1385 (www.revolvy.com/topic/Battle of Aljubarrota). – Tr.

The three of them could not control the smiles that rose from their hearts to their lips, thus sealing commitments that would stretch into the future, which everyone hoped would be prosperous.

After the storm that had taken him to the hospital had passed, the young Spaniard seemed to recover considerably. The nighttime attacks diminished, and he returned to the normal rhythm of his activities, without, of course, giving up the alcohol. It is only fair to state that the abuse created an unfortunate dependency, with unpredictable consequences. His reasoning was sometimes slower, and just one shot of whiskey would make him irrational, even though he said it made him more lucid. Such is always the excuse of the unscrupulous – that cane of support to justify the continuation in vice of any nature.

December had come with Christmas promises and New Year's prospects. Cooler winds blew, announcing that it would be an inclement winter, which was unusual in the area, but which did happen now and then.

The country's political situation was becoming more critical.

Meetings were held more often, and speakers at them were becoming more audacious, as was natural. The regime of shameful exclusion had to end, although it still remained intact due to consent by the great world powers. But the soul of freedom sang fearlessly everywhere, longing to spread throughout the vast heavens toward the future.

Heroes slaughtered in Soweto, the Black city neighboring Johannesburg, became symbols of the campaign for freedom. Children, women, the elderly and young people, who had been the victims of brutality and revenge, in a shameful massacre by troops of the Smuts government, rose up by the thousands, vilifying the barbarism and slavery imposed on them.

The fiery Gospel-based preaching of Bishop Desmond Tutu flogged the criminal social conscience, remembering those who were suffering injustices, according to the teaching of Jesus.[12]

Bishop Tutu stated ardently that we must not repay evil with evil. However, it was indispensable to remain firm in the purpose of the conquest of citizenship, of the right to a more humane and dignified life, considering that the existence reserved for the people in many cases was inferior to that of irrational animals...

He invited the consciences of good men and women to examine the drama of an entire people, of an entire nation that was under the arbitrary dominion of merciless conquerors who had usurped power with guns, reaping hopes and destroying aspirations, curtailing any possibility of moral, intellectual, human growth for the country's inhabitants, nullifying their ideals of life.

He went on to state that history shows that the duration of cruelty is short-lived, because dictators, even when they succeed, do not escape sickness, natural death, or death by accident or murder... including those who seek to replace them on the throne of cowardice. All pass away, and freedom gives the victims of perversity the right to sing and smile, building a better future for their children.

---

12 In the spirit author's Portuguese version of the present work, the following four paragraphs are a direct quote by Bishop Tutu, but no reference was given for the source. The bishop would have originally given the speech in English, and since it is considered very bad form to translate from a translation back into the original language (see The Chicago Manual of Style, **11.92** *The sin of retranslation*, 15th ed.), the paragraphs are rendered here as an indirect quote. – Tr.

The bishop ended by proclaiming that, in the contemporary world, although slavery and indignity thrives wherever the heads of nations subject their people to imprisonment and submission, under the whip and destructive weapons, this ulcerative cancer will be short-lived. The Divinity, touched by the suffering of millions subjected to the abuse and injustice of soulless men, was promoting the arrival of His ambassadors – some of whom were already in the world – to cauterize their wounds and close the heinous cycle that remains. It will not be long before the shackles will be broken and freed hands will work the land of the sentiments to build a new society, a happy people, a humanity free of slavery, discrimination, shameful processes of political and racial persecution, and castes, and women will acquire the dignity that was taken from them, subjecting them to the most vile passions still remaining in the sentiments of men.

More vehement proclamations sprang up everywhere, while the madness of the weak and the sick, thirsting for vengeance, increased the wave of equally unjustifiable crimes and cruelties.

In this state of worrisome prospects, a couple of relatives from Spain arrived at the residence of Manolo and Eneida during one of the country's festive seasons. They were the young Spaniard's cousin, Armando Velásquez, and his wife Clara. Armando was biologically linked to the Rodriguez clan.

Manolo and Eneida both welcomed them exuberantly because they had been recommended by Manolo's uncles, now living in Palma de Mallorca. However Eneida experienced a strange sense of revulsion toward Clara. For her part, Clara did not try to hide the frivolity that characterized her personality, while Armando, a lover of wine and other alcoholic beverages, seemed weary, submissive to his sensual, outgoing wife.

Armando inevitably found in Manolo the ideal pole around which to revolve in his unbridled search for pleasure through alcohol and tormented sex.

Clara was indulgent and vulgar. She tried to tempt Manolo but was unsuccessful because, at the time, he was more interested in transferring the company to his father-in-law and did not want to generate a disturbing emotional situation.

Manolo rebuffed her somewhat forcefully, although he was tolerant of her eccentricities.

At the Latin club on Saturday nights, Clara became the center of attraction. Armando did not seem to mind, as he was accustomed to the woman's conduct, which had long been reckless and perverse.

The truth was that she was not content with her conquests. She had always wanted to be wooed, to be the center of general interest, to attract attention, which she easily did. Since she lacked moral and cultural values, she had become contemptible, choosing to involve herself in scandals.

For Eneida, the woman's conduct was a torment that caused embarrassing situations. During one of these, after Clara had been approached by one of her admirers when the two were shopping in the city's mall, Eneida went home and ordered Manolo to tell their unwanted guests to leave, even before the upcoming New Year's Eve festivities.

"I'm afraid," she said wearily, "she might cause a scandal and create a conflict between vying partners, whom she encourages with gestures worthy of prostitution and debauchery of unparalleled vulgarity."

"Let's wait for the start of the new year, and then I'll send them back to Spain," Manolo replied, concerned.

"I refuse to go out with her," said Eneida. "I don't act like that but it makes me look like I do. My conduct is strict, irreproachable."

"I guess you're right," he wisely agreed, which was unusual regarding the way he viewed mundane acts, though he tried to preserve his wife from any suspicion.

Clara was pleased with Eneida's decision because it meant she did not have to control herself. She could go out by herself and flirt with anyone who merely glanced at her.

Since it could not be otherwise, she attracted the attention of a carefree but attractive young Afrikaner, Hans, who also cultivated sensuality and indecent habits.

At their first meeting, Hans declared to her the lively interest she had awakened in him and his eagerness to win her at any cost.

Stimulated by vanity and driven by ambition, she began to encourage the disturbing affair, offending the people who knew she was married, her almost always drunk husband, and her host family.

Devoid of balanced sentiments, she began going out with Hans in his car and engaging in compromising sexual unions, which became *le plat du jour* for the local gossip. Although the city pretended to be cosmopolitan, it was actually a city where everyone lived in veritable racial ghettos. The Latin ghetto was relatively small, where good morals and family customs were preserved...

Warned by his cousin, Armando smiled confidently, explaining:

"I'm well aware of my wife's conduct. She's always been like that, but she loves me and I love her back. These affairs soon give way to boredom and indifference, and she returns to my arms, thirsting for affection and emotional support... She's a poor girl who was unloved as a child, and now she allows herself the delusion of searching for what she was denied. I'm patient with her and I try to nourish her with tenderness and hope."

"Well, you both need to be gone as soon as possible, because your degenerate conduct is affecting my family. We try to live according to the standards of ethics, morality and dignity."

"Now don't be unfair, Cousin. Have a little patience."

And after a short pause:

"We can't go back to Madrid for now. We have problems there, and that's why we decided to come and breathe the African climates of the South."

"What was so serious that it forced you to leave Spain? Dad must not have known about it, because he recommended you both wholeheartedly."

"Of course not everyone knows about the unpleasant incident."

He cleared his throat to continue slowly, trying to remain lucid despite the dipsomania:

"Clara indulged her behavior with the banker of one of our acquaintances. He courted her cynically and somehow managed to establish a relationship that was deep enough for him to demand that she leave me. I can see why she would want to enjoy herself with those who court her, but I am the love of her life. She turned him down, which generated a lot of friction. What's worse, he too was married and, under the illusion that he and Clara would live together, he had left his own family. That led to a lot of drama and conflict. She decided to take advantage of the situation and asked him for a large amount of money – something easy for him to get – to take care of some problems. But she didn't have the courage to leave me. Without further concern or saying anything to him, we left for Paris in order to entertain ourselves, which led him to despair. We stayed in France for three months and spent all the money on various living expenses, purchases and nighttime entertainment... We returned to Madrid, and now he was the one who did not want her anymore. He felt exploited, filed a complaint with the police, and initiated a lawsuit for fraud, accompanied by extortion and persecution, something we can't get away from... hence the idea of living in South Africa under your protection. You just can't refuse us."

Armando's insolence was so great it seemed like shear madness. The naturalness with which he narrated the venal conduct shocked Manolo, who never thought he would meet someone worse than himself, desirous of climbing on his back to be carried.

Annoyed to the point of losing control, Manolo yelled at him, saying that he would not go along with their depravity and thievery. They were to return to Spain to legally answer for matters pertaining to their ignoble acts.

"My house is not a hideout for criminals," he shouted, raising his clenched fists and slamming them onto the table. "This is all I need. A deadbeat and a prostitute hiding out in my home, which they mean to transform into a brothel to shamelessly and indecently continue their absurdities with my protection and help, dragging my family through the mud!"

He had not yet finished unleashing the fury that had suddenly assaulted him, when he realized that his cousin was about to pass out from being drunk and had not even registered Manolo's outburst.

Furious and unsure about what to do, he discharged his anger by kicking the table and then giving it a shove before heading for the garden, blaspheming and shouting swear words.

Eneida had heard the commotion and came down the stairs from Esperanza's room, holding the little girl in her arms and trying to find out what was going on. She found her husband almost apoplectic, red-faced and eyes bugging out of their sockets...

Manolo was about to continue his show of rage, when the frightened little girl began to cry, bringing him back to his senses. He took her in his lap and gradually calmed down, explaining, still somewhat irate, to his wife what had happened.

Eneida was stunned and understood why she had felt an instinctive revulsion for the wastrel.

"Well, what now?"

"I'll wait for his degenerate wife to return, and then I'll kick them both out."

"Be careful and don't do anything rash, or the solution might become a new problem for us."

After a brief pause, she added:

"I've heard that Clara's present lover, Hans, is a lowbrow and is famous for causing trouble, both in Johannesburg and here. He's already been thrown in jail more than once. He's a deadbeat who sponges off his parents. He hates to work and he exploits women, forcing them to steal to finance his whims... And by the way, where do you keep my diamond necklace and earrings? I'm afraid she might try to steal them just to please her depraved lover."

Manolo seemed struck by lightning at the memory of the diamond necklace, but then assured her:

"They're in a safe place where no robber could ever get to them. If one dared to steal it, he'd pay with his life."

The night had descended without preamble.

The air was stifling, almost unbreathable, a mixture of air pollution and the psychic atmosphere weighing on the intimacy of the family.

After the talk with his wife, Manolo stayed in the entryway waiting for Clara to return, which only happened after midnight, when Hans's car stopped noisily at the door to drop her off. She got out laughing, came up the steps and half-stumbled into the room, where Manolo invited her to a serious conversation, in spite of her deplorable state.

"Your husband is lying unconscious inside. I must inform you that tomorrow, bright and early, you will both have to be out of my home. You have defiled and offended both it and my respectable family with your despicable conduct. I will not have any more patience or tolerance for either of you. So, as soon as you have sobered up, please leave."

Under the alcohol's influence, Clara reacted as if she were in her own house. She defied her host, using obscene language, very typical of her vulgar personality.

Manolo became furious, lost control and slapped her face so hard it knocked her to the ground. A trickle of blood ran out of the corner of her mouth. He stepped forward to attack her once more, when Eneida came in and forcefully stopped him, shouting:

"They don't deserve our sacrifice. Have a little patience because we could end up in a bad situation if we act without thinking. This wench has to go, but via other means. I'd like to get rid of both of them right now, but charity won't allow it, because they deserve our pity. We'll do something about it tomorrow."

By stopping her husband, she had prevented a tragedy of unforeseeable proportions.

He immediately offered his hand to Clara, who was still on the floor, hurt and blaspheming. He helped her stagger to the upstairs suite and laid her on the bed almost unconscious.

It turned out to be a dreadful, sleepless night marked by cruel, asphyxiating nightmares.

The day dawned in heavy fog, blocking the sunlight.

When the two guests awoke with headaches from a terrible hangover, they took showers to try to renew the energies they had spent on the excess of unwholesome pleasures. Then they went down to the dining room for breakfast, where they faced their composed, silent hosts. The light breakfast was eaten in a sullen, unpleasant environment.

Before he left for the office, Manolo went straight to the point:

"When I return this evening, I expect to find you gone. Please pack and then go wherever you want or I'll be forced to call the police and have them deal with both of you, including phoning Madrid and informing them of your whereabouts... That is how we are going to say goodbye, and I hope we'll never see you again because you have defiled this noble home."

Armando did not seem to grasp what was happening. He was acting like a half-wit because his neurons were no longer recording the events around him. Under the stimulus of the alcohol, he would regain a little mental control, but soon would quickly become incognizant. Thus he had no energy to react.

It was Clara who, taken with a veritable nervous crisis, angrily stomped up the stairs and began packing their bags haphazardly while shouting in defiance. She tossed clothes on the bed and then crammed them in the suitcases along with other objects and personal belongings, while knocking over vases and crystal candlesticks that decorated the furniture in the room.

Continuing to shout and uttering curse-filled threats, she telephoned Hans, who was taken by surprise after Clara had given him a quick run-down of events and asked him to come and get them immediately to take them to a hotel.

Hans arrived less than an hour later and was dumbfounded by the number of bags. He put what he could in the trunk and in the back seat, helped the miserable couple get in, and sped off.

The lovers agreed that the ideal would be to go to Johannesburg, where there were hotels in a position to host them, and then think about the direction they should go with their lives.

While Armando remained indifferent, Clara worked out the problems, encouraged by Hans.

Upon arriving in the cosmopolitan city, they quickly found lodging in a good quality hotel. There was, however, the problem of how they were going to pay for it. She considered pawning some of her jewelry until a less upsetting solution appeared. Her idea was immediately agreed to.

The days went by turbulently, invariably wasted on the saturation of the senses.

Two weeks later, feeling tired of the insatiable diva's caresses, Hans decided to propose a different life to her, one that would be rich in emotions and sensations, one that would definitely be worth trying out because of the amount of income it would generate. He suggested that she become a high-end call girl, which would be highly profitable. After all,

Johannesburg was the capital of gold and diamonds, where millionaires went for entertainment in South Africa, as well as to make profitable deals, all the while making trips to the ultra-luxurious casino in Sun City.

She reacted against the indecorous proposal as would be expected. He knew she would react that way at first, but through opportunity and well-developed circumstances, she would change her mind. He was, without a doubt, a capable procurer. He always became satiated with his lovers after having used them for some time, after which he would make them work for him as prostitutes, avoiding any responsibility or commitment to noble work.

Hotel C. was a veritable mine of wealthy idlers. Hans proposed to the couple to move to it, as it would be easier to secure lucrative encounters due to the meetings and parties that were often held there, bringing together vain TV and movie stars – a segment of society that was weary of pleasures, but forever tormented by the need for new ones. The money for expenses, of course, would not be lacking, as it relied on the attractiveness and skills the new Dulcineia had before Don Quixote found her...

The fateful plot continued to unfold.

Hans was skilled in the art of seduction. He would start by using his self-attributed charm, and then would switch to brutality, which he resorted to amongst caresses and threats. After a few days, he secured Clara's first client. This changed her moral category, and she acquired new standing in the decadent society in which she moved.

Armando was indifferent to the whole thing. He just enjoyed his liquor, delicacies and a few flings with other young women who were as emotionally disturbed as he was.

When Manolo returned home and found it devoid of his wretched relatives, he could not conceal his resentment and anger toward his parents. After all, they were the ones who had been responsible for asking him to welcome them in the first place.

Nevertheless, he did feel some relief in returning to live out his own impudent aspirations and to give vent to the torments that inwardly afflicted him.

It happens that, due to their mental band, criminals easily identify those who are like themselves. They fear them because they are aware of their depravity. Even when they meet to engage in nefarious activities, their moral inferiority conspires against unity, causing them to betray each other in order to survive.

Since their souls are marked by their perverse past, they prowl the paths of sordidness, seeking each other out, meeting and hating each other.

Clara, well-managed by her shrewd exploiter, became well-known in the hustle and bustle of vulgarity. She had become an *escort doll* serving depraved old men, who kept her at the top end of licentiousness.

The human heart, however, is a labyrinth of difficult emotional twists and turns, which disturbs even its possessor. Although Clara had become a professional, hardening herself and denying herself the right to true pleasure and joy, stimulated by pecuniary interest and all that money could bring, she could not escape her sentiments. She was young, a dreamer, but miserable because of the husband she had chosen and the specialized lover who was suffocating her in sensuality, which was now causing only disgust and mute revolt. But she could not escape the trap of her emotions.

Such was her situation when she met a young diamond buyer from Antwerp named Fabrice, a handsome, courteous, rich and refined man, who had been attracted by Clara's charms. We can say straightforwardly that she was irresistibly captivating. After a few brief sexual encounters, feeling disposable and profoundly lonely, she fell in love with the seducer, who had let himself be seduced. She did not tell her lover what was happening to her. Tired of being used and troubled by ever increasing amounts of alcohol, she finally confessed to her new companion what was in her soul and asked him for protection.

Emotionally sincere and even regretful for so many follies, she could not open her heart completely but managed to confess:

"I've never really been loved. Growing up at home, I had an unbearable life, which led me to seek a marriage of convenience in order to escape my rich but drunken father and my indifferent mother. I stumbled upon a wretched character – my husband's... Our relationship has consisted of mutual interests from the beginning. He gives me the freedom to help him with his addictions, and I'm free to do what I please, as long as I make money."

"But he's no man," said Fabrice. "He's a worm that can barely think. He's a reprobate. Isn't he jealous of seeing his wife being passed around as if nothing was happening?"

"Not at all. He thinks I love him and he thinks that is why I always go back to him. Actually, I've never loved him. He was a source of security in the traditional society of Spain and was a sort of rudder for me. But as time goes by, I detest him more and more."

With feline skill and intuition, she did not mention Hans. She was afraid that her appeal would not find any resonance in the Dutchman's sentiments if she told him everything.

"I've never met a man who could touch my soul and please my body like you can. I know your business here will be quick and you'll soon have to go back to Belgium. The few days we have together will enrich me with joy, but they'll also throw me into the gulf of longing and future despair."

"There's no point in thinking about tomorrow while we're together and can live our joys, happiness and illusions today. Life is made up of promises, disappointments and slight hopes... It's not worth it to take everything very seriously, especially when it comes to sex and love."

"You speak securely and coldly. You must have suffered some blows to your affections and feelings."

"It's natural that this has happened. No one reaches the age of thirty without having seen their dreams and fantasies turned to rubble, leaving a vast emptiness in their inner world. I myself used to be married. I loved my wife and I thought she loved me back. I only realized later that her sentiments didn't match mine. We were very different people, so living with each other was difficult. We decided to get a divorce. Fortunately, we didn't have kids, which greatly facilitated our process of emotional separation. Any kind of sentimental bond just vanished."

After a pause, demonstrating the seriousness of his character, he concluded:

"I don't plan to ever get married again. I like my freedom. While it's true that a well-structured home is something I really miss and that life as a single is always stormy, due mainly to the fact that there isn't a family, which brings happiness to parents when blessed with children, it is no less true that a good home is, at the moment, very difficult to build, at least as far as I'm concerned."

"Because there's no one who deserves your love and trust?"

"That's right. When sensations make up for them, one's emotions get thrown off balance. Everything turns into satisfactions that don't last... Let's face it: people today are driven by petty interests, and exploiting, using and putting others down. They're always driven to exaggerated selfishness, to pleasure without responsibility, and to money. Nothing else matters – neither the sentiments, nor human beings in themselves, in their condition of humanity. I must say, I'm utterly disillusioned! But let's change the subject."

"I guess I'll have to agree with you somewhat, because not everyone's the same. In the midst of the garbage and slime, in society at rock bottom, there are still good people like you, people who are capable of loving, and they do so even if it means self-sacrifice."

"I agree. I've been looking but haven't found anyone like that yet."

They did not say anything more. They had come to a crossroads of emotions, with each of them thrown into the immoral troubles that made them suffer, pouring out pain and sadness.

Realizing that she might be losing an excellent opportunity to be happy, Clara tried to recover and invited her lover to have a glass of champagne, which he was pleased to do.

When he left, Clara became completely lost in thought, which was unusual for her. She thought about youth, which soon withers; beauty, which wanes; joy, which dies; and illusion, which passes away, and she could not stifle the tears, which flowed in abundance from her...

For the first time she felt the existential chasm into which she had plunged headlong. She was not living in the present; she would have no future... A horrible thought pierced her mind like a devouring ray: suicide! What was the point of a life bound in heavy fetters, a life she was trying to neither see nor feel?

At that highly emotional moment, in the overwhelming, anguishing silence, she remembered God, who, once, when she was a child, had been introduced to her by the dominant religion of her homeland. And touched by its tradition of prayer, she made a fervent plea for His help.

There is no cry of the soul that does not find resonance in the Spheres of Ineffable Love, and, as an immediate answer, help came in the form of a venerable nun who had been her teacher in grade school.

The spirit caressed her tenderly and was moved by the affliction of her former ward. She applied balsamic and rejuvenating energies to her while singing a sweet regional ballad, which she had taught to her beloved students as children of her heart when she was on earth.

Gently, the tormented woman quieted down, the stream of tears subsided, and a reposeful and benevolent sleep came over her.

End of Book One

BOOK TWO

1
THREE YEARS LATER...

Those were tumultuous days because the country was on the verge of collapse. International pressures were demanding an end to the heinous apartheid, and the autochthones had voices that were calling for justice in their name. Bishop Desmond Tutu had won the Nobel Peace Prize, and his message was heard around the world, inveighing against the evil crime of which Blacks in that country were victims. Democratic freedom with equal rights was the only viable solution for South Africa. Nelson Mandela was in prison, but was both respected and feared. Demonstrations were no longer broken up using excessive force, but using methods more compatible with human dignity. There were strikes, rebellions, civil war, carnage, mass murders...

Many foreigners, frightened by the course of national politics, decided to sell their assets and began leaving for Europe, returning to the more affluent countries. This was especially true of the Portuguese and Spanish, who, after transferring many assets and resources to their respective countries on the Iberian Peninsula, planned to emigrate. It seemed like the best solution, saving their lives for the second time, repeating what had happened years before, but now in a much more advantageous situation.

The currency was losing value in international trade, and properties for sale were increasing; and even though prices had fallen sharply, there were no buyers.

Manolo had become more and more misanthropic, aloof, ambitious, and alcohol-dependent. Thus he had become a terrible husband, whom Eneida put up with on account of her own moral and religious convictions. But each day, she became more afflicted.

Manolo's spirit enemies increased their siege and tormented him with the memories of the cowardly acts that weighed on his conscience.

In light of notices regarding the approaching revolution, he decided to transfer the rest of the company to Dr. Henrique Albuquerque and Júlio. He even sold the mansion, under the pretext that he wanted to move to another city.

Consequently, as an emergency measure, he went to live with his in-laws. But something was happening in his inner world. Jovial because it was in his best interests and sociable because it was appropriate, he behaved himself while living with the Albuquerques.

* * *

Clara had succeeded in seducing Fabrice in such a way that she ran off with him to Antwerp without saying anything to either her lover Hans or her husband Armando, whom she left behind. Armando yielded to his alcoholism and slid completely down into the moral swamp, where he would exist in a deplorable state of human decomposition.

Hans refused to accept having been abandoned. He raged and fumed and threatened half the world, but could not find a trace of information about where his mistress had gone. He finally accepted the unfortunate occurrence and sought solace and pleasure in other arms and other sources of income...

* * *

Esperanza was most assuredly a lovely child in both body and soul. Jovial and pleasant, everyone loved her. If her grandparents and uncle were enthralled with her intellectual development, her parents adored her and spared no efforts to make her happy.

She was enrolled in a distinguished school in order to socialize with other children and learn the bases for an intellectual education, in addition to English, Portuguese and Spanish – improving them by communicating in them with her parents in the home – and having a future enriched with blessed promises.

Spring had arrived with a smile, and the whole landscape was decked out in flowers. Fragrances wafted along on gentle breezes.

Nevertheless, one could see that Manolo was quite agitated, but with no apparent reason, since everything was going so well, including his relationship with his wife and other relatives. He had set aside some clothes, shoes and personal effects, explaining that he might have to take a business trip at any moment to decide the family's future. He offered no further explanations.

In the meantime, he and Eneida had been invited to be best man and maid of honor by a friend whose wedding in Johannesburg would be of high social relevance. They prepared themselves with aplomb and Little Esperanza, who was to be the flower girl, was dressed in pink silk and lace, including a wide-brimmed hat adorned with a bright silk-wool ribbon matching her cincture, which in turn matched the outfit the bride had chosen for all the children accompanying her. They traveled amidst smiles and happiness, with plans to arrive back home that night sometime.

The reception afterward was very well organized. After the bride and groom had left, the guests gathered in groups in the huge yard of the mansion of the lucky bride's parents, drinking champagne and wine, and eating from the beautifully prepared buffet.

About 10:00 p.m., Manolo told his wife and daughter it was time to head back to V. He had behaved himself well, avoiding drinking, which was rare. After they had left the city limits, he slowed down and, at one of the highway's major junctions relatively close to the airport, he said to Eneida:

"I think there's a problem with one of the tires; it might be flat. Could you jump out and take a look at it? It's the left rear one."

Even though it was nighttime and the area a bit dangerous, Eneida showed no concern. She jumped out and went to the back of the car to check the tire.

Something extraordinary happened next. Manolo started the car and drove off without her. Frightened, she calmed herself down, thinking he was playing a practical joke on her and that he would be right back – but he did not return.

Desperate and utterly destitute of defense, she was paralyzed with fear, her chest in excruciating pain, and tears pouring from her wide-open eyes.

Happily though, another car came along less than five minutes later and she was recognized by its occupants, who stopped and called to her. They were friends who had been in the wedding and who, finding her in that inexplicable situation, also became frightened and offered her a lift.

Eneida was crying and desperate, unable to explain what had happened. The female friend tried to calm her down, explaining that maybe Manolo had been drunk after all and was not responsible for what he had just done.

The trip resumed in distressing anticipation, during which Eneida was unable to regain her composure.

They arrived at her home, but Manolo and Esperanza were not there. She woke her parents and brother up, and after telling them what had happened, they too were taken with despair.

Obviously there must have been an accident – they thought in dread – for there could be no other explanation for the delayed arrival. They called the police but were told that there was no news of any car wreck on the road. Now, in horror, and unable to understand what had happened, they were beset by uncertainties, and right after the debilitating emotions, their bodies were overcome with torpor.

The day dawned, finding everyone still awake and on edge.

It was then that Eneida found out that Manolo had emptied the closets of his best clothes and most valuable personal possessions – and of course the diamond necklace and earrings, which he had kept at the office before bringing them back to the house – as well as a few clothes and shoes for Esperanza.

It just could not be possible that the idea burning in her mind was true: He had kidnapped his own daughter and had fled! But why?

She presented her conclusion to her mother, who, also frightened, began to consider that possibility.

They immediately contacted some of his family members who were still living in the city, but they said they did not know where he was – a bold-faced lie devoid of any sympathy for the mind-bending pain afflicting the Albuquerque home.

In fact, Manolo had run off to Spain, to Palma de Mallorca, where he had acquired an apartment with the approval of his parents after months of slow, careful planning in secret.

In addition to the ignominious act, he had made off with a large stash of Evangelina's gold coins, having discovered their hiding place with the sharp nose of a hunting dog, thereby adding an economic aspect to the moral damage.

There are plots of cruelty that only high-level psychopaths can devise without the least sentiment of compassion or humaneness.

Manolo had bought plane tickets in advance, and when they had boarded and Esperanza asked where her mother was, he explained that she had been injured when she jumped out of the car, but that everything was fine and she would be joining them later. In his crazed delusion, the schizophrenic's perverse mind had taken care of every detail with cunning foresight, leaving no signs of the treachery he was about to commit.

Of the many daggers that pierced the heart and body of the Albuquerque family, none of them would cause severer, long-lasting pain. It was as if they were all involved in an endless, boundless nightmare that made no sense whatsoever.

Dr. Albuquerque reported the incident to the police and hired a lawyer to find out what measures to take. The whole family suffered the result of a very complex, nonsensical tangle.

The police consulted the national airline's passenger list and found the names of the perpetrator and the little girl. They had flown to Madrid that very night, a few minutes before twelve...

The shock was terrible, and now, since Esperanza was a South African by birth, legal measures had to be taken to recover a child that had been taken abroad without the mother's consent.

One can never know great suffering without having experienced it. The depth of the anguish and the acid that repeatedly burns a mind that cannot find any logical reason for certain human attitudes and behaviors almost always lead to madness those who fall victim to them. Eneida was on the edge of the abyss of insanity. Neither she nor Evangelina would stop crying, while Dr. Albuquerque and Júlio sought legal ways to minimize the drama and find ways to recover the child.

Were it not for their knowledge of Spiritism and the mediumistic communications that provided the lenitive to endure the harshest phase of the misfortune, mother and daughter would certainly have plunged into total madness.

How could one imagine such wickedness in someone who lived, loved and was loved; someone who shared in his family's sentiments? Although the media offers this sort of Dantesque spectacle every day, no one ever believes it will actually happen to them – maybe to one's neighbor or to someone else... But since this is also the reasoning of one's neighbor or of that someone else, it occurs in all homes to all people, save understandable exceptions.

The days were now longer and more marked by bitterness; even if the sky was blue or the night constellated with stars, in the soul of that mother and in the sentiments of that grandmother, there were only and always darkness, desolation, longing, sorrow...

What was most disconcerting was the attitude of the fugitive coward's family members, who hid their knowledge of the brazen act. They withheld any information that might help find Esperanza. The girl was desperate too, after all. She had suffered the loss of her loved ones, and was now in a completely strange environment, experiencing afflictions that would scar her existence forever.

After many days had passed, Manolo and his own, equally imbalanced mother, told Esperanza that her mother had died, that she had been a mental patient who should not even be remembered.

Enrolled in a school run by nuns, with strict orders not to receive anyone or to have contact with anyone who was not authorized in writing by Manolo himself, the child would bear her cruel fate surrounded by strangers. In spite of the benevolence of the nuns and the kindness that some of them showed her, Little Esperanza would never again be the same cheerful, intelligent, happy girl of the past... The mark of sadness, evocative of longing for her mother and grandparents, would remain, keeping her in a frequent state of melancholy.

Manolo had told the nuns that the child's mother was a psychopath that had been involved in witchcraft in South Africa, which is why he had brought her to Spain. The naïve and ignorant mother superior believed him and accepted the fraudulent information as a pretext to save the girl's soul from the wiles of the Devil...

But let us face it: no demon of religious mythology would ever devise a plan and execute it with the heinousness and iciness with which that dreadful descendant of the Rodriguez clan did with the consent of incoherent parents.

This and other ways are how each spirit sets the parameters for its future evolutionary experiences. Being the author of crimes that the scale of justice does not reach to weigh and correct, the spirit inscribes them in the highly delicate mechanism of its conscience, which then programs the means by which they are to be paid for.

None can thwart destiny – although they always try – without grave consequences manifesting at the opportune time, demanding immediate, poignant payment.

In Spain, the wicked Manolo managed to deceive corrupt religious officials, whom he bribed at a high price, stating that he had been a victim of witchcraft and demonic ceremonies, from which he had managed to escape with his life and to save his daughter in the city of V., in South Africa. He then remarried soon after his unforgivable act. Meanwhile, the torment of the Albuquerques continued under the blessings of God and the renewing faith that animated them regarding the future.

Evangelina's psychophonic and clairvoyant mediumship provided moments of peace, nourishing, in the family's suffering hearts and afflicted minds, hopes for better days ahead after the storm, while urging them to pursue legal procedures for annulling the marriage and recovering the kidnapped child.

It was more of a strategy to keep them in good spirits, although the forceful Laws of Life were being kept to the letter, and the potential for immediate peace was very remote, if not impossible, under those circumstances.

Documentation was very carefully drawn up and was sent to the metropolitan curia at the earliest opportunity, explaining the whole matter and requesting that the documentation be sent to Rome for the annulment of the Catholic ceremony. The results, however, were not favorable.

This was not important in the end, however, because the liturgical ceremony had no legal significance in the country. Nevertheless, the Catholic atavism of the Albuquerques demanded that the bond established by the Church be undone, because Manolo had broken it with indignity and madness, remarrying another woman in his homeland, thanks to his own venality and that of the church officials he had bribed.

Private detectives hired by the victims located the poor wretch in his Spanish residence, and there were plenty of proposals that would eliminate him with relative ease, as is fairly normal in the social sphere, where pending matters are handled by murdering the antagonist.

The moral uprightness of the Albuquerques, however, would never consent to such procedures, always opting for measures established by law, as well as by the Divinity. Dr. Albuquerque always remembered the teaching of the Master, when He said that *even the hairs on our heads are numbered,* making it clear that everything happens under the superior control of the Godhead. He concluded that, if all that had happened, there were weighty reasons for it having happened; and with that in mind, he remained trusting in the irrefragable Justice of Heaven.

The blistering pain that visited them remained, however, robbing them of the joy of living and motives for continuing their corporeal existence.

The blessing of prayer and the edifying readings taken from Allan Kardec's *The Gospel according to Spiritism* became the sole precious resources for sustaining their courage and hope, both which seemed increasingly faint as the months passed without a change of prospects for the better.

With the help of friends who lived in Palma de Mallorca, Eneida, in her anxiety and dedication as an abandoned mother, decided to go there herself, under the illusion of being able to see Esperanza, to surprise her during one of the moments when she was being taken to the residence of her father and his new wife, or some other circumstance...

There is always a thread of hope hovering in the broken human heart, like a faint light in dense darkness, offering good cheer.

So, with an expectant soul, she made the trip to Palma de Mallorca and settled there in a hotel next to the girl's school. She would often pass by its outer gate and its surroundings so that at any moment she might see her and know that she was in good health, at least, thus finding a little peace-of-mind. After a week of discrete watchfulness, she caught sight of the child as she was playing in the sun with some other students in an area adjacent to the building. It was all she could do to keep from rushing through the gate to rescue her. She was restrained by Júlio, however, who counseled patience and trust in God, avoiding an even more serious problem with the local authorities.

And she was able to restrain herself, despite being filled with even more despair and anguish at finding Esperanza so close and yet so far away, increasing the affliction that arose from the lack of physical contact, intimacy and tenderness that mother and children enjoy. She wanted to hug her little blond angel, to kiss her cheek and cradle her body against her gasping chest. Nearly numbed by suffering, she let her brother drag her, in tears and very pale, back to the hotel with a look of death stamped on her emaciated countenance...

It was then that a mute hatred exploded within her being against the criminal that had made her so wretched with his smiles, which were actually grimaces, and caresses, which were actually spicules of his disguised perversity. At that moment, she was being consumed by a cruel sentiment of revenge that was building a nest in her mind, ravaging her even more because she had never felt anything like it before.

Knowing that the little girl was alive and relatively well, she returned to South Africa to continue her seemingly meaningless existence.

All attempts to extradite Esperanza failed for some mysterious reason, despite the legal exigencies regarding the matter and the incontrovertible proof of the abduction.

The first year of desolation passed slowly and terribly. Invincible time was in charge of adapting the family to the new order of exhausting events.

Weak and emaciated, Eneida found her only support in her Spiritist Faith and began devoting the best of her time and sentiments to it by studying the Doctrine and finding consolation in light of the incomparable Law of Cause and Effect.

Nevertheless, she would often take one of Esperanza's little dolls in her lap, and as if she had lost her mind for a few moments, she would sing the ballads she had sung to her in the past. Her sweet, sad voice filled the bedroom and was heard outside, bringing her mother to tears. Eneida was not interrupted, for it was a catharsis for her superhuman suffering.

Then afterwards, she would go back to facing the harsh reality.

She transferred her mind to the future, when the adult Esperanza would be able to decide whether to come looking for her or not. She was unaware of the ignominious scheme that Manolo had prepared and executed, trying to erase from the girl's mind every wholesome memory of her family...

Her unspoken resentment toward the traitor went unchanged, slowly devouring her on the inside. When forgiveness shines in the mind and dominates the sentiments, the pain resulting from the most horrific event becomes more bearable than it would otherwise, when the sentiments waste away. For this wretched type of conduct there is no lenitive that makes suffering less wearying. Although such a reaction is never justified, since the perpetrator is actually much worse off than the victim, one could nevertheless understand the behavior of the devastated mother and wife.

* * *

Although the spiritual meetings at the Albuquerque's home lacked a collective character, they eventually attracted a small group of friends that were touched by Evangelina's mediumship and by the excellent topic that is Spiritism. Well-explained by Dr. Albuquerque, it was inevitable that, sooner or later, the Doctrine would awaken the attention of students and scholars of the human psyche to the possibility of the spirit's survival of physical death, a matter that was constantly debated and eagerly studied due to its moral, spiritual, and social implications.

Among the friends who attended and participated in the weekly studies was the Catholic priest João Pedro d'Almeida, a brilliantly intelligent young man of approximately thirty years. He was a polyglot and a great connoisseur of History, someone who tried to live the doctrine he embraced with all the respect and fidelity possible. The fact was, however, that he did not feel much at home in his chosen career – or let us just say, the career that his mother had imposed on him since childhood – for he had not actually been called to embrace it, nor was he unable to escape from it...

He had been born in Penacova, Portugal, a charming town surrounded by luxuriant mountains (because it was at the bottom of a valley, it was known as *pé na cova*[13]) and cut by the Mondego River, which passed through Coimbra on its winding march to the sea. In this town his childhood had been scarred by the needs that assailed his home after the discarnation of his father, a humble farmer who had left behind only a small house and a limited estate, which the widow diligently tended in order to glean the meager resources for her own and her son's living. A determined and fervent Catholic, she had dedicated the existence and care of João Pedro to Our Lady of Fatima, of whom she had become a devotee, to the point of traveling on foot every May and October each year – as was and still is customary in the country, when promises are kept or when devotees simply offer dedication to the worship of love, gratitude and faith. In addition to her devotion to the Church, she knew that if it was impossible to provide her child with a good education, because of a lack of economic resources, he would receive one in seminary and in the religious life, which was, to a certain extent, correct according to local standards.

Young João Pedro thus went to study at the Lisbon Seminary, under the strict auspices of his instructors. He revealed an excellent disposition for the priesthood and expressed the fervent desire to work in Africa after his ordination. His intentions were the Christianization of

---

13 Literally, foot-in-the-hollow – Tr.

the African peoples, to whom the Portuguese Jesuits had committed themselves so much in the past, so he was sent to a small, modest monastery dedicated to St. Francis in the city of V., in South Africa.

The monastery had been erected in a wooded area near the sleepy Vaal River, which watered its own ever-fresh and verdant banks. It was dedicated to the *Trovatore di Dio*, whose life still charms humanity for its sweetness, humility and love, characterizing his indispensable moral values for following Jesus wholeheartedly while supporting the decadent Church of his time.

Under the kind paternity of a Scottish priest, Father Paul-Newton – simple of heart and a dreamy poet, who believed in human beings and who also loved nature as well as the creatures in it – Father João Pedro was in charge of the pastoral care of the faithful Portuguese-speaking Catholics that resided in the city, discharging his ministry with seriousness and integrity.

In his capacity as a scholar, he also taught classes at the college for the descendants of his compatriots, standing out in the community for his honesty as well as for his example of kindness and understanding toward human miseries, whether in the confessional, where he faced the tragedies of daily life, or in the external struggles of social life.

A friendly, excellent conversationalist, when the meetings involving spirit benefactors adjourned, he would discuss them with the Albuquerques and other participants, presenting his views on the mediumistic communications, which truly fascinated him.

It was on one such occasion that his discarnate mother identified herself to the group, including referring to one of her fingers that had been severed while working in the field. The revelation led him to accede emotionally and intellectually to the phenomenon.

"My son," said the happy mother, "today I see and testify to reality; I live it and experience it with other possibilities that I barely had during my earthly pilgrimage. I was a simple woman and did not have the intellectual or financial resources to educate you and make you as happy as I would have wished. As I told you many times while in the *physical world*, I had no other choice but to send you to the seminary. It was not a thoughtless decision but the result of my best and most profound thinking. And I do not regret it; on the contrary, I can see the excellence of the approach you have taken, which has spared you from the bewitching illusions of the world and its follies. You have stayed focused and are worthy of the ministry that you perform with dignity and sacrifice."

After a few seconds of silence, she continued:

"I can understand your struggles as a frail man and the inner difficulties that afflict you due to your vows of chastity and celibacy, which I neither perceived nor understood while I was on the earth. In fact, it takes a lot of effort to stay worthy of such vows, in view of the outward appeals of the world and the inner needs of incarnate beings, especially for those who intend to be faithful, living as they teach others to live, and respecting the vows they have made. But I'm sure that the Lord Jesus is helping you so that your life may unfold in conformance with your choice. I pray to Him always, beseeching Him to bless you, adorning you more and more, so that you will not stumble on the social conventions that challenge you at every moment, nor become corrupted, as is common, by maintaining two forms of conduct: that which everyone sees and that which no one sees, but which you inwardly deny.

"So, I watch over you tenderly with love that death does not extinguish and will never consume. Today I am standing beside your father, whom I met, or rather, who received me at the Gateway to Immortality and helped me take the first steps at adapting to the Home that will one day receive you also, rebuilding our family. I have come here with him and have discovered an entirely new world, specifically with the consent of Monsignor Alves da Cunha, our venerable pastor who broke with the age-old tradition and ignorance to help lives find a safe haven of peace and the lofty experience of their enlightening duties.

"I will return whenever possible to communicate with you, my son, and with the devoted friends of this circle of prayer and spiritual study, from which we all draw inspiration and strength to carry out the commitments we made before the Divine Consciousness. "Since I cannot, nor should I prolong my visit any longer, I ask God to bless you always. I too bless you emotionally, enveloping all your friends in vibrations of health and peace."

When the spirit finished, Father João Pedro's eyes were wet with tears and his heart was filled with happiness. Yes, that was the magnificent woman who had loved him. Everything confirmed her identity: her voice and her refined, determined way of being, although there was a difference in the way she expressed herself. It was now more perfect, which was understandable, given the many years that had elapsed since her discarnation, during which she could have regained the intellectual knowledge that had been blocked during her last existence, or which she could have acquired in her new one...

When the meeting ended, João Pedro had given his testimony, rich with emotion and certainty, complementing the medium responsible for her mandate, for which she was a trustworthy instrument and deserving of the utmost respect.

When comments were made concerning the message, João Pedro stated that the issue – chastity and divorce – was very painful to him, considering how young he was and considering the organic forces that demanded immense control and even sacrifice through austere moral discipline, inspired by the guidelines of the Church itself.

* * *

At today's level of culture and civilization, it is no longer possible for castrating, medieval behaviors to continue to guide lives based on erroneous data manipulated by tormented individuals of yesterday, who, ignorant about the sexual functions, considered them to be *dirty* and conducive to sin and crime, and detrimental to one's religious existence by giving way to wild and pernicious behaviors.

Human beings were born to love and exercise their sexuality to the utmost within the principles of ethics, morality and societal life, performing its functions in a dignified, lofty manner.

The basic function of sex is procreation; even so, due to the hormones connected with it, it is endowed with highly meaningful emotional purposes, triggering sentiments when engaged in appropriately.

No one can repress human nature without suffering unpredictable consequences, especially in the areas of emotion, thought, organic functions and conduct.

A so-called sin always exists in the mind of the one who commits it, and not in the act per se, because there are individuals who keep themselves *pure* only on the outside, while going through disturbing experiences on the inside, which end up unbalancing the nervous system and mental orientation.

The baseless, antiquated religious prohibitions derived from the prepotency of human leaders who were responsible for punishing society for the crime of aspiring to the happiness that they themselves – masochistic tormentors that they were – could not enjoy for one reason or another. They were concerned only with prohibiting, punishing and persecuting others instead of dedicating themselves to guiding, teaching, leading and loving, and letting people live their own lives in the best way possible while respecting the law. Slowly, because they are aberrant and aggressive toward freedom of conscience, movement, citizenship and behavior, such guidelines and requirements are collapsing shamefully into ruin, where pride and arrogance used to predominate, and which still want to prevail, but without any moral support to vitalize them.

Human beings advance along the paths of freedom, in the direction of responsibility and respect for the duties that mark life in all its aspects.

* * *

Thus it is understandable that the comments that night focused on the scabrous act of prohibiting the noble function of sex.

Dr. Albuquerque was well-versed in the subject and used the happy occasion to elaborate on the decision he had made while a priest in Angola, choosing marriage instead of continuing under the urges of stormy passion and pretending to be someone who was immune to the sexual function and better than other people, unlike some psychopaths who believe that they can find refuge in religion, hiding their innermost torments or trying to give the impression of being predestined, superior to the common biotypes.

He spoke with confidence and good judgment:

"The matter of sex in the clergy is as serious as it is in any other social group because of the prohibition and *brainwashing* to which seminarians and priests are subjected throughout life, inducing them to immoral behavior behind disguises that are incompatible with true dignity. Any arbitrary imposition is deadly for human sentiments, especially since we are all very different from each other, whether from the physiological or the emotional/psychical point of view. If there were freedom of choice, general conduct would surely be different, for each could choose that which is most compatible with his own resolution. There would be countless candidates who would opt for preserving their chastity and, by extension, celibacy, thus remaining respected by the flock to which they have devoted themselves. There are many clergymen who remain celibate, but not chaste, which is shameful and inexcusable.

"I will say it again: it was thus by pondering and knowing my own positive and negative moral and emotional values that I chose marriage, rather than continue to embrace behaviors incompatible with my conscience, something I found daily among my colleagues in the priesthood.

"I chose to marry, to break my vows, but to not leave the Church, which resolved to expel me from its roster, even though it was I who asked to leave. It excommunicated me, even though it retains countless members who condemn themselves, while adhering to the standards of faith, which they say they espouse, but which they actually disregard with cowardice. I do not regret what I did, but I thank the good fates who inspired me and encouraged me to make the decision.

"Those who settle for the false security that comes from religion shamefully submit to its unreasonable demands because they are afraid *to face the world and its depravity* – as we have become accustomed to believing it to be. They believe they won't be able to survive on the outside, including the persecution suffered by those who resolve to follow the noble attitudes of freedom.

I must confess that I did not find any misconduct on the outside which I did not find in the sacristy, in the seminary, or in my contact with friends and colleagues, because problems lie with the human being and never with this or that situation or circumstance or place."

He continued his wealth of comments concerning the fascinating subject, addressing the ongoing revolution in the field of ideas and human conduct, especially in what refers to the indissolubility of marriage, interpersonal and social relationships, inviting understanding about the growth of science and of cutting-edge technology, both which have unmasked the most secretive corners of the ancient mysteries.

Father João Pedro had brought Father Manuel Cerqueira da Silva to the gathering to introduce him to Spiritism – which was completely different than what he had heard about it – and in light of the considerations regarding the highly important topic of chastity and celibacy, he could not restrain himself. Very moved, he said:

"As incredible as it may seem, my sexual initiation happened while I was in seminary, while I was living with those who were supposed to teach me discipline and continence."

He paused for a moment because of the delicacy of the theme, and then went on:

"After I was ordained a priest, and accustomed to heterodox practices, I could not keep my abstinence for very long and ended up connecting with a member of my congregation who seduced me right there in the confessional. Unfortunately I did not have the moral resources to withstand her advances, because I myself encouraged her...We have kept a hidden, tumultuous, insecure, hypocritical relationship, whereas we could live together normally, giving vent to our desire to have a family, without fear of the punishments with which we are threatened... I think about it all the time and she has been pressuring me to regularize our situation or she will leave... But I always object, asking her how we would live, since I do not have another profession that would give me enough income to support a home."

"And that is the weapon used by the so-called ecclesiastical superiors," said Dr. Albuquerque: "Keep those who have fallen into their well-laid traps chained to their commitments. They are also afraid that having a family will affect the stability of the clergy, because of labor laws that require the granting of rights to the survivors of breadwinners, in that they would continue to receive the benefits they had enjoyed. Hence the problem of inheritance and of other gains won by the classes that fight for society."

"I feel the same way," said Father João Pedro. "I think that, to defend the absurd position, petty interests are at stake regarding real property and other assets, which would have to be passed on to the descendants of priests after their death, and not to the Church, as is always the case... The patrimony of the Holy See is untouchable, and it is managed by groups of inclement executives who are supposed to increase it, but who have nothing to do with the religious doctrine. International business interests have generated an increase in the fortunes of companies that are supported with the money collected all over the world, but which should be used for works of benevolence, charity and love, as per the determination of the Galilean Master."

"That's far from happening," replied Father Manuel. "What we see is the insatiable thirst for more power and greater greed, while the *children of Calvary* die, starving and sick, by the millions, in spite of an abundance that is not even turned into crumbs to lessen the cruel need annihilating their bodies."

"But new days are coming for humankind," said Dr. Albuquerque, "when constructions not built by the Father will crumble, because they do not rest on the rock of truth, but lie on the shifting sands of corrupt, perfidious temporal powers... In that far-off, yet promised future, however, a mentality more in keeping with the thought of Jesus Christ will spread like a solar light all over the earth, and the material temples of ostentation and cruelty will collapse, with *not one stone left standing...*

"Well, let's go into the dining room for a little snack. Your presence and the heart-felt comments from those who participated have been a real pleasure."

2
TORMENTED, AIMLESS SOULS

ather João Pedro became a frequent guest at the Albuquerque residence. Not only was his interest in mediumistic phenomenology and the content of Spiritism growing, but also his interest in Eneida's placid beauty, wrapped in the delicate veil of melancholy.

He found sincere friendship there and could let himself be carried away by the enchantment the young woman inspired in him; a field for spiritual observations and enriching dialogues, whereas in usual social groups, futility always prevails. Such groups are an escape from culture, which is slowly replaced by commonplace, secondary interests, besides slanderous comments and unfounded suspicions.

João Pedro was aware of the distress that was disturbing Eneida and he would strive to draw her out of her silent, troubled interiorization. Thus, whenever possible he would try to get her attention by broaching religious themes of resignation and courage, two qualities that characterized the special lives of the saints and martyrs.

On one occasion he found her in deep thought in a pleasant corner of the beautiful garden. She kindly granted his request for permission to sit with her and talk a bit.

The soft evening breezes were blowing and the roses in the garden exploded in red, white, and yellow, spreading their fragrance all around. Everything comprised a special circumstance for a declaration of repressed love.

Touched but unaccustomed to the emotions of affection, João Pedro said:

"Loneliness is one of the most painful challenges of human existence."

"But it's less cruel than the betrayal that causes it," Eneida replied bitterly, "especially when it is combined with an evil abduction, like the one in which we were the victims."

"Quite true. But if we can understand the imposition of destiny, we can acquiesce to its terrible, purifying purpose, which ultimately becomes a blessing of deliverance."

"I agree. But no matter how hard I look for a reason for the insane Manolo's cowardly gesture, I just can't find a plausible explanation. I keep visualizing the scene when he asked me to get out of the car to see if anything was wrong with the tire... There wasn't anything on his face that betrayed his cowardly intention of leaving me at that hour of the night in a deserted, dangerous place, possibly at the mercy of criminals. I'm now certain that he did it harboring the desire to put an end to my physical existence right after the act that destroyed my soul."

She could not continue and burst into thick tears that inspired compassion, tenderness, and affection.

The somewhat distraught João Pedro asked her not to give in to despair, asserting:

"By letting yourself be consumed by his cruelty, you're doing exactly what he wants. Crucifixion, so to speak, is a way that makes it possible to rise toward heaven, because, with the arms stretched out, one is verticalized in the direction of the Infinite. But to take flight, one needs to pull out the nails that hold one to the wood of immolation. As long as that's not the case, the pain is always poignant and unbearable. It rends the flesh of the soul, which cannot recover."

"I just can't forget. The cruel trauma of his running off is stuck in my memory. I keep seeing the car leaving me there. With my soul in anguish, I thought he was just playing a practical joke... Later, I waited for him to come back with Esperanza, but that didn't happen and it has become suffering beyond what I can bear. I dream about that moment; I go over it a thousand times in my head, but I can't understand all the disgrace involved."

"In the lives of all of us, things happen that we cannot fully understand until after the death of the body, when the spirit enters the arcana of Immortality, grasping knowledge about the past and unraveling all its implications."

"That is the conviction that keeps me going. It helps me as I await the uncertain future, in the hopes that through reincarnation I will find the reason for the heinous act of such destructive depth. I must confess that if I had not found Spiritist knowledge, I would have given in to suicide, because, in addition to my distress, I don't find any reason for continuing my bodily existence."

"But you know that all religions see suicide as the most cowardly act possible, entailing the most tragic consequences and unspeakable spiritual suffering that human beings foist on themselves."

"Yes, I know that; however, since the Catholic Religion doesn't offer me any moral comfort, especially given the corrupt attitudes of some of its representatives, driven by money rather than guided by evangelical sentiments, when it comes to the annulment of my revolt-plagued marriage, I would rather defy the laws of the Church's arbitrary and unjust God and end it all. Not even the love for my mother, my stepfather and brother would stop me, although they would be devastated. Even so, from time to time I feel like I'm going crazy, and in my delusion, the idea flashes like lightning through my mind... But I would never actually do it. Based on what I've learned, I'll wait in the Spirit World to be reunited forever with my little one."

"Why don't you think about yourself once in a while so that you can wait to reunite with your sweet angel here on earth after this karmic stage has passed? If you let yourself be overcome by the poisonous fumes of resentment, your life might be reaped before its time, and you won't enjoy the happiness that God has reserved for you for later... Actually, it's already time for you to renew your heart with love; to experience joy in order to adorn Little Esperanza's heart with feelings of happiness when you do meet again. Oftentimes, love is close by, singing in our hearts, but we refuse to see and hear it."

"I will never love again, at least in this incarnation. That bastard destroyed everything that was beautiful, good and rosy in my inner world. Whenever I remember his cowardly smile and deceitful caresses while he was coldly planning the destruction of me and my family, I don't think I'll ever allow myself to be caressed again, to feel the warmth of affection, or the tenderness of someone else's love."

"Not all men are the same, and neither are all women. Some are noble and tender, faithful and refined – like you; others are perverse, shallow and contriving... The problem isn't about sexual polarity; it's about each person, according to his or her moral behavior and stage of evolution."

"I have no doubts about that. Unfortunately, with a few exceptions, of course, I'm looking at the world and other people through the lens of my suffering, the endless drama I'm going through."

There was a silence pierced by the pulse of hearts beating in different rhythms. While Eneida was full of anguish, Father João Pedro, though slightly shaken, was hopeful. He had never expressed his innermost sentiments to anyone. But this was the moment God seemed to have given him to disclose himself to someone who just might understand him. So, reticent and measuring his words, he said:

"I've been thinking a lot about my vows to the Church. After that message from my mother so many years after she talked me into joining the priesthood, and knowing that she now has a higher degree of understanding of human beings and of life itself, I have begun to feel free of this awful subjection. I've always wanted a home, the honor of being a father, the blessing of a family, where, after coming home from work, I could experience happiness amid smiles and loving kisses. I now know that happiness is the goal for everyone, although we all have our own vision of it."

He faltered, fearing what he meant to say; it almost took his breath away. His throat was burning, as if by a great thirst:

"I would give up everything if I could join mine to the fate of a woman like you, someone with virtues and lofty sentiments... I must confess that, ever since I met you, something different has started to populate my thoughts and dominate my emotions. I couldn't figure out what it was at first. I've experienced immense well-being every time I've come to Dr. Albuquerque's home. I used to think it was all about just being with the family as a whole, about the Spiritist studies and the profound conversations. But then I discovered that, besides all those other things, you were the main reason for my intense emotions."

Eneida was taken by surprise and did not try to hide the astonishment written all over her face. But she did not say anything, which allowed him to continue:

"In my mind I take you wherever I go. I dream about you being at my side. I long for the joy of being able to talk to you, to feel you close to me... I don't want to keep this sentiment tucked away – I mean loving you in the silence of my heart and not in the open. I just want to hear from you if I can cherish the hope of being loved by you in return so I can make the tough decision to free myself from the cassock... You don't have to give me your answer this minute. I suggest you talk to your mother while I present my plan to your stepfather, so we can securely take the next step."

"But my marriage hasn't been annulled by the Church yet. I'm still technically married."

"Well, actually you're not! Since Manolo abandoned you and married another woman in Spain, he has in fact restored your freedom. He has broken his commitment to being faithful, disrespecting the sacrament through which he is supposed to love you and be by your side 'until death do you part'... Also, you and I would have a civil marriage, according to the laws of this country, but we would be blessed by God just the same. So it wouldn't be a hindrance, but a stimulus for your life to continue within the objectives established by God."

"I don't mean to get your hopes up, and I have to be honest with you, my dear priest. I must confess that what you've told me has taken me by surprise, because I don't feel anything for you other than the sentiment of true friendship. Your presence is most pleasing to me, and you've captivated me fraternally, but there are no other emotions on my part."

"I knew that would probably be the case. But now that you know what is going on inside me, you can adapt your thinking to a different view of me. And that will alter the awful pain you're feeling. I know that I can win your heart, and even if I don't have the economic resources to give you the comfort you're used to, I'll make up for it with my dedication, faithfulness and endless loving support. It's only natural for you to be surprised by what I've told you, because I've tried to disguise the intentions of my soul in order not to frighten you or seem like an exploiter who has not actually appreciated the respect and consideration I've been receiving in this wonderful home."

"What matters to me in love is the love itself, not the things that go with it. I used to live in a comfortable home, but because of the terrible partner I lived with it was never really a home... So in a decent relationship, what you have is not what is important. It's what each person is, each person connecting deeply and enriching the other with priceless blessings and happiness. I can't even think about getting married again right now. Please forgive me and try to understand."

"I'm in no hurry. In fact, I did not expect anything less from your diamantine character. We'll have opportunities to get to know each other better, to give you time to think about it, and to put our minds on another level of emotion. God will decide our future."

Father João Pedro was red as a beet, whereas Eneida was white as a ghost, almost transparent, not knowing what to do right then.

She was flattered, and somehow compensated by feeling capable of inspiring love despite her heartbroken state.

It was Evangelina who, providentially, appeared in the garden and found the two young people silent, immersed in very different reflections, not knowing what to do at the moment.

Spontaneous and benevolent, she could not hide her curiosity:

"What's the matter? Why are the two of you so quiet? Young people always seem to have so much to talk about!"

Then she added:

"Oh, I know. It's the magic of the evening. In my beloved Angola, when the day was blushing in the twilight and the breezes were whispering the soft melody of the coming night, a sweet melancholy would take hold of me, stilling my words and sentiments, and letting the festival of nature take over. The dusk would slowly dim and the stars would come out, inviting me to pray and behold the silvery nests twinkling in the Infinite, where life surely pulsates in other manifestations of beauty and harmony, without the anguish or suffering of earth."

Inspired, she approached with a faint smile, sat down on a wrought iron bench beside them, and seeing Eneida still pale, held her cold hand and gently warmed it between her own two, encouraging her to come out of her ceaseless grief:

"We must forget about evil, my child, so that we can think only of the good that will take us in full one day. Look up at the sky and consider the dimension of time. How many years has it taken for that ray of light to come to us, only reaching us just now? How many of those stars will eventually *burn out* in the wake of the infinite?... Many, indeed, have already gone out, at least regarding their initial composition, even though the light they used to emit has been traveling for centuries, for millennia, only now being detected by our poor eyes. I always remember that my spirit friends have told me that the sun, which enriches us with life and warmth, is the very same sun that warmed the Divine Benefactor during his pilgrimage on the earth. Its rays, which strengthen us and synthesize the chemical substances in our bodies, are the same as the ones that shone on the march of Moses and the Hebrews through the desert more than 3,500 years ago."

And pausing briefly in order to continue to be inspired by her spirit mentor, she concluded:

"Nothing is at the mercy of chance as a fortuitous occurrence with no real reason behind it. The One who conceived and created the universe; the One who gives life to the worm that crawls on the ground; to the virus that has some purpose in the context of life; that One has also mapped out our existence, establishing laws that impose themselves regularly, impelling us forward on our unending advance. The wicked, the weavers of tragedy and misfortune, who now delight in their own madness, shall not escape their own conscience. What we are suffering today because of them, they will have to face tomorrow – though we do not wish it on them – from the sowing of the thorns and disgraceful deeds they left behind, which will sprout and reappear with all the spines that have remained on their paths. Life is eternal, and we are the weavers of either happiness or misery. It is possible that, somewhere in the past, on a night rich in harmonies like these, we ourselves colluded to lay inconceivably terrible plans that reaped other people's lives. Today, fortunately, bathed by faith in the future, and grateful to God for inviting us to make amends, we are reaping the bitterness we inflicted on our neighbor back then. So let us be of good cheer, and not faint in the struggle that has just begun, inviting us to enlightenment and endless joy."

She took the trembling young woman on her lap, as if she were still a fragile and needy child in tears. But her tears were now tears of mental comfort; the dilution of a toxic grief needing exteriorization in order to vanish from her sensitive soul.

Silent, Father João Pedro was also moved by the beauty of her rational faith, logical belief in God, and unrestricted trust in His designs.

The natural silence was interrupted now and then by the onomatopoeia of the triumphant night.

After a few moments, Evangelina invited them to go back inside because the cold wind could damage their health.

The dining room was charmingly lit. The light spread outward from appliqués and candelabras set on the furniture, as well as from a virtual festival of polished crystal chandeliers, in contrast to the darkness outside.

Dr. Albuquerque and Júlio had come down from their quarters after washing up for dinner. João Pedro had been invited to join the family for a while longer.

Feeling welcome and still overwhelmed by the unusual emotions that assailed him, he agreed to stay for the meal.

Eneida excused herself to get ready, feeling less downcast and somewhat relieved of her usual despair. Such crises of self-indulgence and disenchantment were recurrent, and her watchful mother would strive to wrest her out of the depressive state, which is always a bad counselor for those who suffer, as it inspires solutions that only complicate matters rather than solve them.

Dinner was dressed in alacrity filled with comments about the highly significant social events and difficulties being experienced at the time in the country shaken by threats of revolution and by increasing crime...

* * *

In Palma de Mallorca, the always-restless Manolo was gradually being overcome by his usual conflicts, along with the remorse unconsciously lodged in his being. He had also resumed his drinking habit.

After a time of euphoria resulting from his well-planned and well-executed escape, and continuing to enjoy the harm he had caused his wife and her family, without even knowing why he had done what he did, he eventually settled into a routine that stemmed from a life devoid of emotional sense and the vigor of responsible labor.

He was now an investor in the stock exchange, as enthusiastic as always, ambitious to accumulate money, grow richer and enjoy life's concessions.

Without Eneida and her family being aware of it, he had kept his assets separate from hers from the very start, out of fear that he would have to share them. Thus, his mad pursuit of power continued, sure of the fact that even though the marriage was still in force under the laws of South Africa, Eneida would not be able to claim possession of anything of value immediately or even later. His shrewdness would also be his ruin, however, as is always the case with the wicked and insensitive.

His new wife, Olga, quickly grasped the eventual failure of their marriage. She could foresee the slopes of suffering that would come with time. For her part, it had not been a choice involving love. She was divorced and had significant traumas from her first marriage, but had found it very difficult to adjust to being single. When she met the young man from South Africa, she got involved with him, letting herself be seized by his ease of seduction and his arrogance, accompanied by his loquacity when he would tell her of the experiences on the distant continent from which he had come. Some of his stories, no doubt, were more the fruit of imagination than of reality. Even so, it was fun to hear him tell them.

Pampered by the young suitor who enveloped her in affection, perhaps by transferring her numbed sentiments and by the need to find a new social group, she had finally yielded to his courting and accepted his somewhat hasty marriage proposal.

In the beginning, the relationship was rich with illusions. There was no lack of expensive gifts, strolls, trips, enchanting nights in luxury hotels, and casinos filled with those who were passionate about gambling.

The wedding was not magical, but it was quite meaningful. He had presented her with the diamond necklace and earrings, which she could proudly show off at civil and religious ceremonies, provoking envy and awe. It was undoubtedly a set of precious stones of great cost and great beauty.

For his part, Manolo could not escape the fascination the jewelry exerted on him. Before the marriage, he had locked himself in his apartment countless times and let himself be moved by the cool glow of each polished gem. He had memorized where each one was set and the delicate forms they composed as a whole. He also remembered the age-old tradition about ill-fated jewels. Whether they had some magical power or not, the truth was that he was not content to just contemplate the set – he had to hold it, to heft its weight, and to feel its coldness.

Less than six months after the marriage, Manolo asked Olga for the privilege of keeping the pieces in his private safe at the office because it was more secure than the one in their home, which was easily accessible to thieves and domestic employees, especially housekeepers, who always took notice of what was in the homes where they worked.

Olga nodded in earnest without suspecting a thing.

Of course, emotionally he needed to have them close-by, pulling the same stunt as when he had only halfway given them to Eneida.

Whenever he was by himself, fascinated by the "solidified stars" imprisoned in their strong yet delicate settings, he would think about giving them to Esperanza when she came of age. But at the same time, contradictory emotions afflicted him with a peculiar type of jealousy.

The sweet but sad Little Esperanza had been forbidden to ask questions about her mother and the rest of the family ever since she was told about the accident that had taken the life of her mother, who, according to her father and grandparents, did not deserve to be remembered due to her odd behavior before she died.

Meanwhile, Manolo continued to feel great tenderness for his daughter. She made him feel calmer, as if she were enveloping him in an indefinable magnetism. On the last weekend of each month, he would bring her home from the boarding school. He would feel less oppressed and would recover his spontaneous joy, which without her he only felt while drinking. During this brief time he was gentle, and would go for walks with his wife and child, enjoying the delights of wading in the ocean and buying trinkets with which he tried to nullify the blow to Little Esperanza's life and soul after having separated her from her mother.

As if it were an unanticipated divine punishment, as the child grew she displayed the physiognomic features, intonation of voice, and a few other traits that were very typical of her mother, whose image was fading from her memory, replaced by the kindness of the nun in charge of her strict education.

There were times when the evil doer would look at her and be hit by a shock to his nerves, seeming to see his wife again, tortured by his cruelty. But he would change his attitude before he could be accosted by remorse.

During normal activities he continued with the same manipulations that are always used by those who want to get what is best only for themselves. He felt that everyone was capable of being bought and then discarded. He measured the character of others by the weak moral fiber that constituted his own. As a result, he slowly associated himself with a group of skilled stockbrokers, some of them known to be unscrupulous fraudsters. They traded particularly in questionable securities that the strokes of luck promoted during the daily auctions. Thus the cycle of profits and losses always yielded fattened wallets for the manipulators of stocks and other valuable papers. Concomitantly, taking note of the sleazy side of many fortunes, as well as of their possessors, Manolo had no difficulty taking part in the high society of appearances and the suspect business dealings in which many reveled. His own interests involved getting more and more, while caring very little about where it came from.

Without realizing it, however, he became involved with a group of Mafiosi very well placed in local society, who moved large sums on the New York, Paris, London, Frankfurt, Barcelona and Madrid stock exchanges...

Everything seemed to be going beautifully. But boredom – one of the most perverse opponents of all those whose life is not structured or maintained in dignity with lofty goals – began to creep into Manolo's inner landscape and, to escape from himself, he took unrestrained pleasure in joining in the extravagances of his fellow crooks.

C'est la vie! – he would say to himself, without any sense of dignity.

As a result, the relationship at home began to deteriorate and the marriage became almost unbearable for both spouses. Manolo's alcoholism had a negative influence on his behavior. He displayed a marked psychotic tendency, which caused him some problems as a result of regrettable occurrences with his new friends, who, although corrupt, knew how to hypocritically conduct themselves at get-togethers, especially when family members were present.

Such society, which lives by appearances, is responsible for the moral cancers that make the planet a prison of suffering for billions of victims. The leftovers thrown out due to the waste of ostentation; the delirious lust that derives from egotism; the sordid and unconfessable interests that are cultivated – all are factors that generate socioeconomic misery, the offspring of moral misery, which causes some to lose hope and others to go mad, driving them to commit the worst crimes imaginable, with an attitude of contempt for their own life and that of their neighbor, producing incredible psychological escapes from reality, which drugs do not correct but only make worse. Consequently, we see culture, ethics and civilization as a whole plunging headlong into the abyss of the dissolution of customs, toward a bleak future for upcoming generations.

Were it not for the sacrifices of millions of heroes, anonymous or not, who have committed themselves to constructing the good through study, work, struggle and selflessness for the ideals of human evolution in the areas of science, technology, art, justice, religious faith, etc., there would be nothing but despair, as is the case with all those who are emotionally fragile, lacking any moral values regarding the unjust and absurd confrontations that arise at every moment.

Although they feast at rich and exotic tables, whether in luxury or extravagance, these usurpers of the common assets that life has put at everyone's disposal – requiring those who are better supplied to assist those who follow in the rearguard of progress – wallow in nonconformity and desolation, because, devoid of worthy purposes, they lapse into the very lunacy they seek to disguise.

On one such occasion, when too much alcohol made the young Spaniard more talkative, he revealed to some of his friends how life had required him to make sacrifices to arrive at his current situation, but that he had been blessed enough to spend a large sum of money on a diamond necklace and earrings.

Manolo could not restrain himself as he described the fascinating jewels, revealing the avarice that tormented him, as well as the love that bound him to them, arousing greed and envy in his equally sordid dining companions.

One was a mocking and sarcastic Ramiro Alvarez, who challenged him to present the treasure. He accused Manolo of just boasting, a trait common to every *nouveau riche* who loves to brag about what he cannot prove.

Vanity, that special child of arrogance, is a great enemy of human beings, for, connected with selfishness, it rejoices in producing enchantment with its exhibition, providing emotional compensation for the insecurity and imbalance of its victim.

Such was one of the characteristics of Manolo's behavior. Feeling accused of lying, he invited Ramiro to visit him at his office in due course, when he would have occasion to confirm what he said.

He immediately experienced a strange repulsion for and deep resentment against the cynic, who had tried to demoralize him.

Unfortunately, criminals are highly sensitive to the suspicions of their cohorts and they give in to the reactions of animosity that are common to them.

Ramiro Alvarez was of the same moral carat as Manolo – an excellent enemy in a conflictive relationship.

3
THE SHADOW OF THE CRAZED VICTIM CRIES OUT FOR JUSTICE

Ramiro Alvarez was a spendthrift and a cocaine addict. Almost a social parasite, he invested in the stock market with few of his own resources, but had gotten rich through unscrupulous financial transactions. The friends who knew him did not trust his bravado and well-nigh avoided him because they knew that he was an exploiter and a scoundrel. Manolo had not been part of the group as long, so he had not yet had the opportunity to get to know each of its members very well. Consequently, he was about to become the victim of Ramiro's stupidity.

Let us confess that Ramiro had a hidden dislike for the young showoff. He could not understand why the good fates were being so generous toward that dandy, Manolo, and not him. He was thus nursing a sickly, inexplicable envy that was getting worse.

It turns out that the Portuguese loan shark, whom Manolo had Mayuso murdered, was still following the former, waiting for the chance to come down on him with his dagger of vengeance. He felt that now just might be that opportunity. Having found resonance in the psyche of the coke addict, the Portuguese began to transmit his aversion for Manolo, inspiring Ramiro to steal the jewels that had once been a source of truculence and misery for him.

The result was that Ramiro began to foster an unusual, untimely interest in the rumored jewels and want to see them right away. As soon as he thought it appropriate, he sought to confirm the reality of the braggart's information by approaching Manolo under the pretext – the fruit of his ingenious imagination – of a significant market reversal that seemed promising.

When he went to visit Manolo at his office, he presented him with a fanciful plan for purchasing negotiable securities in Barcelona, with the possibility of later transferring them to New York. The securities were decreasing in value at the moment, but would start increasing before long, according to news he had from proven, reliable sources.

Presumptuous, but not stupid, Manolo refused to participate in the deal because he preferred safer investments for now. Besides, he did not have the required funds.

While sipping an aged whiskey, Ramiro stated *en passant*, making his tone of voice as natural as possible:

"You said something to us about a set of diamonds. That aroused our curiosity because we know that South Africa produces some of the purest ones out there. And of course, considering your socioeconomic position, you must have chosen the clearest stones possible – flawless and of excellent quality."

"But of course! My pieces constitute a dazzling ensemble that continues to amaze me due to their magnificence, as well as the superior polishing, which gives them special distinction and value. Just so you can get an idea of what I mean, the set is currently worth more than $150,000."

"Oh, wow!" Ramiro exclaimed. "So it's an invaluable treasure in the form of a very special piece of jewelry! Of course I myself do not possess anything like it, but I must confess that I sure would like to own something of that carat. I take it that your life as an immigrant in South Africa was very successful, taking into account the resources you've acquired, starting with jewels that are as expensive as they are stunning."

"Well, yes, I did work hard and I did live quite comfortably, but the struggles and sacrifices weren't small or easy."

There was an undisguised explosion of pride and pretense in his voice.

"So tell me: why did you move here to Magaluf, to this area of Palma de Mallorca?"

Blinking his eyes with cunning and wickedness, he continued before receiving an answer:

"Any problems with the law, the family, the business – or all the above? I think it's sort of foolish to abandon a treasure trove when everything's going so well..."

"I think you're overstepping your bounds," the other interrupted abruptly. "What are you driving at?"

"Sorry. I didn't mean anything bad by it. It was just a way of talking."

The visitor perceived that his host's life story held some dastardly secret, because his sudden anger pointed to something very serious that lay in the substrata of his behavior. This pleased him somewhat because he knew that, in the history of many fortunes, the presence of ill-concealed crimes, dishonor and sordid debts are nothing new.

Manolo was visibly irritated and was about to ask the overly curious fellow to leave, when, very cunningly, Ramiro stoked his vanity.

"I sincerely congratulate you – a man who is still young; a winner with a bright future ahead of him and a past of hard work rewarded by comfort today."

He made a psychological pause to measure the result of what he had said, and then continued:

"You know, I've always had a special fascination for diamonds. I'm drawn to tales of treasures bearing blessings and curses, and wrapped in myth-laden legends: like the one about the tomb of Pharaoh Tutankhamen, which might have caused the deaths of Lord Carnarvon and all who took part in the excavations of the famous tomb and its transfer, first to Cairo and then to London... It's now almost certain that the pharaoh's ghost, which struck them all so unexpectedly, was actually infectious bacteria and micro-organisms for which there were no specialized treatments at the time, such as penicillin and streptomycin. Even so, it's fascinating when it comes to blood diamonds, those that end up victimizing their owners."

Mentally guided by the Portuguese, Ramiro penetrated the unconscious mind of Manolo, whose thought processes were almost equivalent.

Manolo became interested in what Ramiro was telling him and there was a moment of intense affinity between the two, as if a fateful attraction were bringing them together, carrying out the cruel conspiracy.

In the spontaneous silence, one could hear the beating of disordered hearts, victimized by anxiety or taken by the morbid vibrations of the discarnate enemy.

The spirit Antonio Manuel de Alcântara e Silva had finally found the ideal psychic simile to enable him to get the revenge he had hoped for. Ever since the long gone days of his murder, his existence in the spirit world had centered on the yearning to retaliate. Crushing the bastard who had robbed him of his body, money and those diamonds was what kept him breathing and maintaining the idea of survival. Yes, he was reaping bittering suffering as the result of his former, completely undignified existence, the fruit of the hatred of the discarnates whom he himself had robbed via the exorbitant interest of his dishonest profession, listening to the curses and experiencing the hatred of the widows and wretches who were devoured by his greed; nevertheless, his mind was fixated on his own murderer...

"When the time seems right," Ramiro said in his almost melodious voice, "I would love to see this priceless matching set, if you wouldn't mind too much. Of course it is not a matter as to whether you actually own such a treasure, but rather the natural interest aroused by your information about it."

That was all it took for Manolo, with his chest full of emotion, to ask Ramiro to be patient while he went to get the velvet case that contained the fabulous stones.

He got up and went to an adjoining room, subtly accompanied by Ramiro's covetous eyes. Manolo did not get the door closed all the way and it remained slightly ajar, making it possible for Ramiro, still seated, to watch him as he made his way to the wall safe hidden behind a priceless Lurçat tapestry...

Ramiro stood up furtively to watch Manolo open the safe and take out a large case wrapped in thick navy blue cloth. He closed the door without locking it, and returned to the room where Ramiro was waiting anxiously, but with the appearance of tranquility.

His mind was incited by the crazed discarnate avenger, and an unfelt sentiment of hatred ascended from his heart to his brain, nearly making him want to kill Manolo right then and there.

Manolo unwrapped the box with almost sensuous emotion and opened it.

The two heads bent over the necklace and earrings glittering with a cold light that dazzled them and elicited an exclamation of excitement. Both were pale and trembling.

The magic of the brilliance fascinated them.

Manolo took out the necklace with obsessive care, held it to his chest, and made a motion as if he were examining the display in an invisible mirror. Pride and happiness were evident in a perfect mixture of passion and madness.

Ramiro asked permission to touch the delicate piece in order to feel it physically. Manolo conceded and when Ramiro did so, a strange sense of ownership come over him, as if he had found something he had lost, and which was suddenly within reach. Through his stupefied mind flashed the idea of gaining ownership in any way possible. The obsessor took control of Ramiro's reasoning, urging him to grab the treasure from its illegitimate owner and flee. Ramiro felt as if he were about to pass out.

As the equally cunning Manolo looked at Ramiro, he picked up on his evil thought, and abruptly jerked the necklace away, smiling and asserting:

"It has magical power! It fascinates everyone who touches it. Before you fall in love with its splendor, it would be best to put it back to sleep in the safe, its place of security and peace."

He was shutting the case, when Ramiro, taken by the discarnate enemy, stammered:

"I would almost give my life to own a set of stones of that carat."

"Well, I almost had to do that myself... It cost me a price beyond its appraised value."

He did not mean to, but by evoking the scene that had culminated in the murder, he had attuned himself to the hate-filled victim, forming a psychic triangle of perturbing interchange. The fluids emanating from the mind of the Portuguese enveloped both men, throwing them out of balance, thus generating an unusual emotional disorder.

The afternoon waned slowly. The office was deserted. The warm, stifling air caused them to weaken, providing a special climate for what was about to happen without warning.

Ramiro, fearing that he would never again have access to the jewelry, was literally overcome by the obsessor's energy and threw himself on Manolo in an effort to grab the case.

Manolo had picked up on Ramiro's thought and defended himself with the swiftness of a cat, beating Ramiro and throwing him against the office bureau. Ramiro suffered a cut on the face and fell to the floor. The blood ran hot.

Furious and unbalanced, under the command of the perverse mind, he took a massive crystal paper weight and threw it at Manolo, who ducked, causing it to strike the wall, leaving a dent.

The two of them traded punches and kicks. Since Manolo was younger and more agile, he broke away, grabbed a sharp letter-opener from the table and stabbed Ramiro repeatedly, causing him to explode in cries of desperation before finally collapsing, covered with blood and begging for mercy. Manolo was possessed and would have killed him, were it not for his pleas.

The would-be murderer left him lying on the floor, put the jewels back in the safe, and returned huffing and puffing. In spite of the hatred that dominated him, he helped the fallen man sit in a chair. Manolo then brought a damp towel and handed it to him to press against his wounded forehead and chest. Although the amount of bleeding was not abundant, it was significant, so they decided to go to an emergency room in order to avoid something worse.

"What happened to me was crazy," said Ramiro in a restrained voice. "I've never felt anything like it. An evil power took over my mind and desperation threw me against you."

"Don't worry about it," Manolo replied, still angry. "The necklace is still mine and that's what matters. You'll tell everyone your side of the story about what happened, but I expect this to be the end of our relationship."

"I'm not going to tell anyone. We can tell the staff at the hospital that I was the victim of a street robbery and that the thug took off."

It is certain that saying the event had happened on the street would not arouse much attention, because such attacks with knives and revolvers had become normal even in broad daylight. To the degree that cities become famous and preferred by wealthy individuals, they attract various kinds of thieves and common robbers, who prefer them due to how easy it is to commit crimes, especially when they become havens for careless tourists who are always dazzled by everything they see.

The arrival at the emergency room was uneventful. The explanation seemed to convince the physician on duty, who decided not to notify the police, because the victim said he did not want to be involved in a scandal and that he intended to continue treatment in a private clinic. Hence he was discharged soon afterwards, since his injuries were not serious enough to require immediate hospitalization.

Afterward, Manolo returned to the office. By then it was nighttime. He tried to tidy up the place, putting the furniture back in order and making sure there were no characteristic telltale signs of the fight such as bloodstains and broken objects...

Everything seemed in good order, so he decided to go home. He was physically worn out after the emotion of the incident, whereas his mind was full of questions about the stupid move by the strange visitor.

He could not explain why memories of the death of the black man who had tried to steal the necklace and, later, the planned murder of the Portuguese had both returned to his mind. But when he recalled the latter incident, he felt nauseous and a sudden malaise assailed him. In his half-giddiness, he thought he could see the rancorous ghost of the enemy threatening him. In his mind, as if pierced by a dagger, he heard a laugh followed by a terrible threat, as had often happened in his nightmares. He wanted to scream, but his voice stuck in his throat. He stopped the car and seemed torn from his body, facing the fury of the cruel pursuer.

"You may have escaped from your wife and her family, you bastard," the discarnate rasped angrily, "but you will not escape from us, your victims. We failed this time but we will try again and again until we achieve our cherished goal, which is to bring you here to where we are."

A loud, mocking laugh caused Manolo to wake up sweaty, frightened, trembling.

He could not believe it was the unhappy spirit of the Portuguese, who now presented himself with more strength than ever in order to torment him. He was hostile to the belief in immortality, despite his professed Catholicism – which essentially rests on the immortality of the soul. Faith never seemed to matter to him in the world he meant to conquer, a world which was more important than the advent of bodily death.

In his delirium, he thought that such incidents derived from his guilty conscience, which seemed unjustified, because it would imply that, although the murder had been illegal, it had been moral due to the moneylender's exploitation. Since he had felt devoured by the exorbitant interest that he had imposed on him, and since he knew that he had wished to take possession of his treasure, it had been completely justifiable to get him out of the way...

Olga was very concerned when her husband got home. The pallor on his face reflected his inner tumult.

Solicitous, she asked whether something troubling had happened, but Manolo reassured her with a kind reply and then sought help from a glass of whiskey at the elegant bar of their luxury apartment. After a few well-savored sips, feeling the stimulus of alcohol in his bloodstream, he decided to shower and then rest for a bit before dinner at home.

It had been a while since he had enjoyed his wife's pleasant, benevolent company. The social club had been his favorite hangout in recent months because of his ambitious forays into the stock exchange and the competition amongst those interested in stocks and other assets.

During the meal, the conversation revolved around day-to-day frivolities, somewhat lessening Manolo's emotional tension.

When they had finished with a good digestive liqueur, Olga was pleased to accept Manolo's invitation to sit with him out on the balcony, which offered a view of the immense blue sea.

He silently immersed himself in thoughts that had not occurred to him for some time.

Because of the guilt that he sought to stifle in his agitated mind, he rediscovered the excellence of the home, of the family he had deserted.

Automatically, he remembered Eneida and Little Esperanza, and was almost moved to tears.

Olga observed him in silence, also moved. She still loved him, despite his strange conduct of late.

Soothed by the alcohol as he digested his meal, the images of his former wife and his little girl populated his thoughts, resurfacing by the miracle of memory.

Why had I assumed such a terrible attitude against the woman I still loved? – he asked himself. How could I have planned such a heinous crime, leaving her on the highway at night in a dangerous area, hoping she would be murdered? And, by extension, since I loved Esperanza so much, why was I punishing her by killing her mother in her heart and mind and isolating her in a school that is almost a prison? Why such wickedness?

He began to feel like a real monster, completely disgusted with himself.

In that natural trance of his awakening conscience and the implacable remorse that spares no one, he was seized by a strong torpor which caused him to partially disengage himself from his body in the same way as during physiological sleep. He was reeling from the alcohol, and the emotions and conflicts he was experiencing. In this state of mental confusion, he perceived the venerable figure of a priest, who held out his hand to him and said:

"I am Monsignor Alves da Cunha, who used to live in Angola."

"Yes, yes, I remember your name. I heard it mentioned at the residence of my former in-laws."

"I have come to answer the questions you have just asked yourself. Your crimes have escalated and have become a devouring monster that will soon vanquish you with its vicious, destructive jaws. Rebellious and cruel as you are, you deserve neither compassion nor respect. Nevertheless, the Lord of Life does not desire the death of the sinner, but rather that of the sin. You have been acting detestably and you know it! But love, compassion, mercy and new opportunities for offenders like you never cease. You cannot go back in order to undo or erase your crimes, but you can at least repair their gravity. Return the little girl to her mother, who is going mad with pain and longing, and you will rehabilitate yourself somewhat."

Even under the magnetic action of the noble Spirit, the rebel tried to react, to refuse. But he did not have the strength to express the perverse feelings pervading his personality.

The spirit visitor continued serenely:

"Listen carefully so that you may understand some of the reasons why you avenged yourself on the family that received you as a son, brother, friend and partner, and tried to destroy it in your insane fury."

While this was happening on the spirit plane, Olga realized that Manolo had entered into a calm and refreshing sleep, and decided to leave him alone for a few minutes in order for him to recover.

The kindly spirit guide continued, explaining to the astonished criminal:

"Before donning your present personality, you wore different carnal clothing. Reincarnation is the Law of Life, and not just a fanciful belief formulated by deceivers and people who dwell in the past. The spirit is eternal in its essence from the time it is created by God. It experiences many bodily existences in order to acquire knowledge and to develop sentiments, enabling the divine spark within it to expand and acquire plenitude, by which process it reaches the relative perfection reserved for it. Throughout this evolutionary endeavor, each experience is either a gain or a loss, which it must understand and value, improving on those that are positive, while correcting, through the actions of love or the mechanisms of suffering, those that are harmful. None can avoid this process indefinitely, even if they want to. Indelible as the laws of electricity, gravity, and magnetism that prevail in the universe, the laws of reincarnation constitute the sublime mechanism of God's Love for all, with equal blessings to overcome the evil that prevails in the animal nature of human beings until angelhood at last becomes their normal condition."

So that Manolo, still stunned, could grasp the contents of the priceless information, Monsignor da Cunha paused in a timely manner, and then proceeded:

"At the turn of this century, you, Eneida and Little Esperanza lived a trouble-filled life in Cape Town. All three of you were born there and possessed a great fortune in gold, land and diamonds. You and Eneida married and received Esperanza as a daughter of body and heart. Life's ups and downs continued in your marriage, but Esperanza was the bond that united you both, helping you to overcome the normal difficulties of living.

"You yourself were insatiable and rebellious, always interested in extorting more from others, accumulating more money and enjoying power in the province; hence, you neglected your family and domestic responsibilities, becoming a true tormentor of your wife and a negligent father for the little girl. You were both devoid of faith, because religion comprised a social behavior in your church, thus neither of you had any moral or spiritual resistance against the trials and tribulations that were meant to enlighten you. In the absence of such indispensable support for exemplary conduct, you surrendered to the dissipations that money and power provide, while, in your home, Eneida and Esperanza, basically abandoned and imprisoned in the golden cage of the ease provided by wealth, were being consumed by resentment and a lack of love, which would culminate in emotional disaster for all three of you. You, yourself, indulged in venal, offensive and licentious behavior involving shameful affairs, with no regard for home or society. Hypocritically participating in associations that pretended to care about customs, you were incapable of correcting your sexual aberrations or your addiction to alcohol.

"It was in that atmosphere that another man approached your wife, a man who was worthy and felt sorry for her in her abandonment. He beckoned to her with promises of love and freedom, which ended up captivating her and relieving her of her unhappy life with you. It is true that this was not lawful for her to do. Nevertheless, you yourself were responsible for the affair, and like I said before, since you did not have the moral strength to resist the temptations of pleasure and the seductive world, she left you, taking four-year-old Esperanza with her...

"Crazed with hatred and jealousy, you – who did not have the right to demand one bit of respect from her – took legal measures to get your daughter back, and you created evil plans for revenge. However, you were unable to carry them out, because death approached you through liver cancer, the consequence of your foolishness, and you left the terrestrial proscenium to harass them with your insane spiritual pursuit."

The narrator paused again to give Manolo time to internalize the timely information. Sweaty and anxious, his gaze was far off because, as he was listening, he was reliving the scenes that were stored in his deep unconscious, and he could better understand the facts to grasp the inexorable Law of Cause and Effect.

Monsignor Alves da Cunha continued:

"Death, which always reaches all individuals in order to resolve problems that they put off and refuse to solve, took the others also, and years passed amid suffering and aggressions in the Sphere of Immortality. Since there are always new opportunities for restoring paths and repairing damage, you were each called to reincarnate in turn so that mutual love and respect could help you make reparation. Eneida found affectionate hearts from other past incarnations, individuals who received her with inexhaustible affection and have sustained her emotionally during this great night of pain. One of them is the man who supported her back then, and who is helping her overcome destructive conflicts, but now as her biological brother, Júlio. Do not be surprised by the affection and understanding they have for each other. There is nothing perverse or unhealthy involved. You often unconsciously recognized the one who had taken your wife from you, and you experienced morbid jealousy, forgetting that it was he who facilitated your reunion with her at the Latin club, providing you with the opportunity to make amends, which you wasted.

"What did you do instead? Crazed and wretched, with no reason to be that way, except for your unconscious thirst for revenge, you back-stabbed the one person who could lift you out of your moral chaos and exiled your daughter amongst strangers, in a false pretext of religious education, but lacking the responsibility of her own family, which is always the best school possible – when its members become masters of healthy habits and upright behavior.

"And do not think N'Bondo and the Portuguese, whom you murdered in such a cowardly manner, are foreign to your existence. Among the crimes of your previous life, you plundered much of the property belonging to Antonio Manuel de Alcântara e Silva, who, in turn, harmed you in this life with the exorbitant interest on the money he loaned you. It is a recurring plot between exploiter and exploited, when love and compassion should hold sway, modifying the structures of behavior and molding the sentiments of each of you for the better. Now, in addition to the terrible murders you perpetrated by bribing other individuals, you have missed your opportunity with Eneida, whom you swore to love and protect, and Esperanza, who is an orphan of living parents, and whom you harmed with deceitful, outrageous information regarding the memory of her worthy and faithful mother.

"When are you ever going to wake up?! When are you going to realize that, even if you do not mean to be, you are headed for your death, because the journey is unavoidable?! How can you remain asleep while wanting more and more, you, who have squandered other inheritances and have taken possession of assets that do not belong to you? Wake up, Manolo, and start over... There are plots against you on both sides of life, and in the future it is doubtful that you will have the luck that has just saved you from the loss of the necklace and your physical life. I am your spirit friend along with others who advise you, but we cannot go beyond our limits, especially since you neither cooperate with us nor with yourself.

"I know that upon awakening you will say that this meeting was a vague dream, nothing more. But I will be at your side striving to remind you, giving life to the words that will be imprinted in the depth of your being. You still have enough time to start over, to make amends. If you miss this opportunity, it will be too late. See you soon, my careless friend!"

The venerable figure faded away before the wide open eyes and the gaping mouth of the spiritual patient, who soon awakened in the gentle breeze that blew in from the sea.

He tried to figure out where he was, and automatically remembered the dream.

Still lying on the chaise lounge, he began recalling a few of the experiences revealed under the inspiration of his spirit friend and became preoccupied with the interesting phenomenon.

He remembered the presence of the austere cleric and the particular incident regarding the information about his past existence, which presented itself to the degree that it was narrated, as in a movie. The scenes resurfaced amid the complexity of the events, demonstrating their truthfulness.

Meanwhile, he experienced a virtual frisson of experiences regarding his inner world.

Nevertheless, in his skepticism of spiritual truths, he tried to identify the factors that might have caused the altered state of consciousness. He thought that perhaps it was due to the conflicts of that afternoon and, after stretching, to take in more oxygen, he was still somewhat fearful as he climbed into bed for the rest of the night.

Human beings who are unequipped with moral values always seek to escape reality, altering occurrences at will, so as to avoid responsibility. These psychological, invariably unconscious escapes are responsible for a significant increase of foolhardiness and imbalance. It is always more convenient to believe that events were meant to happen as they did, thus avoiding any commitment to rehabilitation and the righting of wrongs, rather than consciously facing them, weighing their meaning and their consequences.

Since reality is indestructible, only a few existential circumstances can be altered, and in the future they resurface more vigorously with heavy burdens of nontransferable responsibility, summoning the foolish to confrontation and repair.

4
MENTAL LANDSCAPES RESULT FROM THE ACTION OF EACH CONSCIENCE

Manolo, always both irresponsible and insensitive, threw himself on the bed and fell into a deep sleep. Now, without the beneficent assistance of his benevolent guide, he had to face two enemies beyond the physical realm who had become part of his existence – the Portuguese and N'Bondo.

He could not hide the terror that gripped him when he saw the deformed and disquieting faces of the two discarnate enemies. He could tell that he was not dreaming, but was actually there with them in person.

He wanted to get away from those disturbing presences, but he felt himself bolted to the ground, sweating profusely and becoming immobile. He was able to think clearly, but he could not define what was happening to him, for his limbs were dominated by terror, making him incapable of any kind of movement, except the prolongation of despair.

"Well, do you recognize us, you bastard?" asked the Portuguese, who presented himself completely enraged.

His hatred was unequivocally obvious, and he expressed it all as if he were a demonic spirit, as portrayed by the religious traditions of different peoples. But he looked like a devilish being that had been, or who still might be, human.

"In your cowardice, what made you think you could silence us when you destroyed our bodies?" he asked, gritting his teeth.

Bulging red eyes, a twisted face, and a gravelly, almost unintelligible voice, comprised the commanding being that faced Manolo.

"We are not your conscience, because you don't have one. Instead, we are what you made of us with your heinous crime, which no one has found out about, but from which you have benefited so much. But you shall not go unpunished, for here we are, and we have come to charge you for the debt of our lives. You ruined the family that gave you affection and respect, so that you could continue with your accursed fate, accumulating an impressive heritage. But you won't be bringing it here with you when you die, no matter how attached to it you are. You've had a thousand chances to rehabilitate yourself but you chose to stay wicked, cynical and disloyal, as if the universe exists only because you're alive. Where are your sentiments? What have you done to them? When Cain, the son of Adam and Eve, faced God after murdering his brother Abel, he bowed in shame and repented. You're worse than he was because you still thirst for blood, and if you were given another opportunity to murder someone, you wouldn't hesitate for a minute... We'll show you the same mercy you showed us. N'Bondo's home was destroyed and his children reduced to poverty because of you, and he became a monster who lost his ability to think. His thoughts are thoughts of revenge, of your destruction ... We mean for you to be here with us, in this world where no one can hide behind the mask of shamelessness, as you are doing there on the earth.

"Get ready to pay, you bastard."

Then, with hands clenched, the spirit advanced toward Manolo, who was twisting and turning in bed. He cried out in despair and woke up numb with terror.

Olga had not yet retired and came running at the sound of her husband's desperate voice. She arrived to see him, unconscious, trying to get up in a state of astonishment before falling out of bed onto the floor completely out of his mind.

She tried to get ahold of him to help him up, but as if instinctively wanting to free himself from the invisible hands that meant to strangle him, he resisted at first, but then managed to calm down little by little with the help of his distraught wife.

She gave him some fresh, comforting water, spoke softly to him, wiped off his sweat, and wrapped him in waves of tenderness, as only love could do.

Now composed, Manolo took a deep breath, regained his usual cynicism, and explained:

"I'm being hounded by demons..."

After a timely silence in order to gather his thoughts, he continued:

"As I was resting peacefully out on the balcony this evening, I dreamed of a famous Angolan priest, who came to warn me and give me advice about a lot of what I have done. His words were kind yet severe, and were very beneficial. As he spoke, I experienced a wonderful mental phenomenon that made it possible for me to see what he was referring to. When I woke up I was ready to face the day, even though I was still tired."

He paused again and continued:

"But then I went back to sleep and felt I was in a strange, dark and terrifying place, being visited by two demons that presented themselves as two actual individuals I knew when I was living in South Africa. They were threatening to kill me. Although monstrous in appearance, they had some traits that enabled me to identify them. One of them, in particular, a famous loan shark full of rage, came and wrapped its claws around my neck. That is when I awoke in terror."

"It was just a nightmare. Sometimes they're the result of worries or emotional stress and they're released by the unconscious in a terrifying manner," said Olga in an attempt to reassure him.

"Well yes, but they always entail something grounded in actual events that took place in the past."

And after a brief reflection, he added:

"I'll put a stop to these hallucinations tomorrow. I'll find a psychiatrist or a psychoanalyst – whichever will best help me recover my serenity."

He had scarcely finished telling Olga his plans, when he heard – he could not tell whether it was within him or on the outside – a shrill laugh followed by the usual threat:

"That's what you think, you bastard! We shall make you pay your entire debt to us, coin by coin."

Manolo quickly went pale and began to shake like a leaf, concluding, terrified:

"This is an emergency; I must be going mad."

Confident about the success of their plan for revenge, the obsessors foresaw the distress they could inflict on the soulless fellow, concluding that they would soon have him completely in their hands.

For the Rodriguez couple, that was a night of restlessness and anxiety.

* * *

It just so happens that one cannot escape oneself. External situations of life are masked; real events are denied; worthwhile investigations are thrown off course; disgraceful deeds are covered up – and the applause of a consumer society is won. Nevertheless, it is impossible for the inner being to coexist with the outer one, the real being with its hypocritical personality. The occasion always arises in which inner values awaken, and the dichotomy between what actually is and what is presented produces a split in the personality, which opens the field to disorders, some of which are seriously depressive, others psychotic, and others hallucinatory. Hence, if a healthy coexistence between the spirit and the external world in which it lives is not possible, the flight to conflicts and deviations of conduct becomes unavoidable, generating tribulations that could have been mitigated by means of the harmonization between what one aspires to and how one conducts oneself.

Human beings are severely lacking in a healthy religious belief molded by personal experiences, one that would give them a global view of life, its essential goals and its secondary goals, one that is set on the future they choose for themselves as individuals through their behavior.

Nevertheless, a new dawn of faith will break in due course, the kind of faith embodied in the experience of spiritual reality, when legitimate mediumship, put in the service of exchange between the two vibratory bands of life, will lead to an understanding of earthly existence within ennobling parameters, and not through the illusions of the arbitrary senses, giving the false idea of a perpetuity that does not exist, due to the consumption that the physical organism undergoes.

When human beings become aware of the fact that they are essentially spirit and not a physical envelope, they will begin to live according to the highest standards of justice and equity, love and charity, disentangling themselves from the primordial passions to have the enlightening and liberating experiences reserved for them to foster their unending moral ascent.

Spiritism has undertaken this glorious task, although it has been delayed because of the indecision of many of its adherents who have not internalized the liberating postulates that comprise the Doctrine.

* * *

The extensive sufferings afflicting the moral and spiritual economy of the Albuquerque family led to greater unity among its members.

The home meetings involving the study of the Spiritist Doctrine were enriched by philosophical analyzes and scientific discussions of its postulates. And the study of the moral and spiritual consequences that should be reflected in one's daily behavior was not neglected. Activities involving charity became a bright project for helping the poor, especially those whose lives had been reaped because of misery and the prevailing prejudices.

Everyone who participated in the weekly meetings had discovered weighty reasons for continuing their existence. A strange sensation of the peace and joy of living nourished them as special blessings, for they had discovered the treasure map of happiness, whose guidelines they would follow until they found the fortune reserved for them.

After the edifying discussions, there was a brief time for prayer and meditation, when mediumistic communications through Evangelina occurred.

The serene and lucid words of Monsignor Alves da Cunha, along with concepts presented by other high-order spirits, answered questions, shed light on complex texts, and opened new fields of commentaries that could edify the participants with spiritual agape.

Having been enlightened by knowledge pouring forth from the Most High, they would sit in silent meditation to benefit from energies sent to them by their tireless, discarnate tutelary spirits.

The environment was saturated with wholesome fluids, enabling the members of the group to linger a bit longer amid helpful commentaries while being served refreshments or coffee, in keeping with salutary social habits.

Time, on its inexorable journey into the future, left pain-filled events in the past, never to be revived, except in special situations, when someone had information that might comfort the family about Little Esperanza, who was developing both physically and mentally according to correspondence from friends in Palma de Mallorca, or when there was news about Manolo's emotional health.

Eneida had lost a lot of weight as a consequence of an almost complete lack of reasons to go on living. She had only managed to do so because of her faith in Divine Justice and the hope – admittedly remote – of finding out what had actually caused her insane husband's devastating attitude.

Slowly, however, at the insistence of family members, particularly Júlio and her mother, who did everything they could to help her distract herself a little, she abandoned her self-absorption and began taking part in group conversations again.

Because of her suffering, her opinions certainly were sensible and on the mark when the theme focused on human problems and conflicts, demonstrating that, without reincarnation, there was no logical reason for facing life's difficulties and challenges.

"Reincarnation," she once said confidently and emotionally, "is the most prodigious good that Life offers to evolving spirits on earth. It eliminates the fanciful conceptions about certain individuals being blessed by grace to the exclusion of almost all those who are deprived of that divine concession. Moreover, though reincarnation may be severe, it is completely fair because it applies to everybody on their progress toward perfection, giving them the same experiences, lessons, trials and expiations, by which they purge themselves of the wrongs they have committed, so they can resume their endeavor of self-improvement and inner renewal."

When invited to give her opinion, and after overcoming her natural shyness, she would become visibly inspired, acquiring a seraphic beauty that overcame the weariness showing on her face.

On one of these occasions, someone who was rather insensitive, though without malevolent intentions, asked her:

"From the perspective of reincarnation, how do you see the drama that you yourself have been living these past years?"

Without hesitation, though with a slightly flushed face, Eneida explained serenely:

"There were more than a few days and nights in which I was immersed in the painful events that have enveloped my present existence, that of my daughter and that of my family, events caused by the insensitivity of the man I chose to be my husband. There were times when I felt like I would go mad, and I cannot hide the fact that macabre ideas of revenge occurred to me, such was the hatred burning within me. I felt I could take the sword of justice in my hands and try to kill him myself, or pay a hitman to do it for me. What sense did my life make after he had destroyed it? – I would ask myself. After having gotten my revenge, I would also put an end to my own journey... But then I would think of the burden of suffering that would befall Esperanza, who would have to bear the odious memory of one more tragedy added to the first – she and all those who loved me and shared my sorrow! That instantly caused me to change my mind because I do not have the emotional constitution to make others suffer.

"However, it was the logic of reincarnation that guided me onto the path I have been following, giving me the strength to reflect: Either there is nothing at all, for everything is the spurious fruit of chance, or there is God, an order to the universe, a Law of Cause and Effect that rules everything. Since chaos cannot generate equilibrium, nor can nothing produce everything... well, that leaves only one option – that of a Divine Creation, the Intelligent Causation of life and all occurrences. Understanding that the earth is a school and not a *vale of tears* – despite tears being shed in any school – I wondered if the remote cause of the evil events that enveloped me might not be within me myself.

"I saw my husband as a psychopath because of his mood swings and changes in behavior without any reason... His hostility toward loved ones, even toward his biological family, grabbed my attention, and often I feared for his strange demeanor, which I was somehow able to manage. I saw an almost continuous crazed look in his eyes, the presence of a sick jealousy, a morbid distrust, and I wondered where these impressions came from... Why did he love me and at the same time despise me? Since then, I have come to understand that some perturbing memory had remained stuck in his unconscious, reaching his lucid consciousness without the clarity needed to identify it."

Eneida paused to better concatenate her reasoning and express it lucidly.

Those who were listening to her were attentive to her explanation of the drama they had never dared to question her about.

With luminous eyes, as if a distant and powerful light were shining in them, she continued:

"One night, when I was thinking about my little girl and was at the door of madness from missing her, I felt a pleasant breeze. It tranquilized me, and I fell into a torpor somewhat different from physiological sleep. In this altered state of consciousness, I felt I was on a verdant mound as evening fell amid a halo of colors. The *voices of nature* seemed to be silent in order to allow me to hear the soft hiss of the gentle breeze. Enthusiastic and moved, I felt led to pray. I had never experienced anything like it, and I don't think I will ever experience such precious moments of ecstasy again. I had no thoughts, nor did I have to have any. As I prayed, there were no words; there were just feelings flowing from my heart and mind, like waves of multicolored lights surrounding me and widening around me, making it possible for me to hear music reaching me majestically from some unknown region.

"In the dazzling light, I suddenly saw an angelic being, smiling and affable, transparent and luminous, who advised me: 'Bless the pain tearing at your sentiments! All affliction, all suffering results from the selfishness and disrespect that one's spirit allows itself before the Laws of God. Above all things there is always sovereign Divine Justice. So great is such law that nothing happens by whim of chance. Consequently, it must be trusted. The crown of glory can be donned only after the battle is won. Never distrust Heavenly Providence. Have courage before the crucifixion that is being imposed on you, for it is just. This is not the first time that you are in the world with the one who is wounding you to death today. Forgive him and forgive yourself so that your burden of affliction may be less heavy. Jesus was innocent but did not complain or try to justify himself – he forgave everyone. The night's storm brings benefits to the sun-drenched daybreak, making the atmosphere lighter and more transparent. Happy always is the one who redeems, who suffers, who trusts and loves.'

"The angel came closer and, touching my forehead, invited me with energy: 'Now, behold the reason for your suffering.'

"It felt like there was a whirlwind within me, and I was able to watch, in an instant, the entire unfolding of a lifetime, as if it were alive and pulsating in my brain, in that area of the spiritual memory that had been touched. I was able to relive that unhappy experience, when, under his lash and cruelty, I had no strength to resist, so I abandoned him in a terrible way... It was I, therefore, who had unleashed the ferocious storm that now came over me.

"I was dismayed with myself, but the happy sensation soon returned. Even so, I no longer enjoyed the tranquility I had felt. The venerable being concluded: 'Now that you know why you are suffering, take heart, continue in the good, and trust in God. Nothing justifies the crime of revenge. Even though you wronged him and your home in that lifetime, his hateful deed in this one was not justified. God does not need human beings to do his justice; rather, in their haste, they always choose revenge, despite being asked to forgive. That is your case right now. Never consider revenge – it is not yours to exact. Love overcomes all matters and manifestations of evil. Love always and suffer courageously, totally surrendered to God. He watches over you and all, including your enemies, as a loving and watchful Father.'"

Eneida paused again before concluding with emotion:

"The sublime spirit who had come to my rescue faded away before my tear-clouded eyes, leaving an unforgettable fragrance in the breeze blowing over the landscape, now turning into starry night... and I lost consciousness. When I awoke the next day, I told the rest of my family about the phenomenon so that we would all be trusting, forgiving those who, in one way or another, had become our tormenters in the present, and promising each other we would not broach the matter again, except when summoned by God.

"So, in short, that is how the key of reincarnation explains the enigma of the awful events that caught our whole family unawares. We see our persecutor as being a wretched psychopath who deserves compassion rather than resentment.

"Without a logical reason to justify the anguish and pain that bring ruin on human sentiments, rebelliousness and despair disorient those who experience such afflictions. They feel helpless when they see the joy of others while they suffer this terrible injustice themselves. Any one of us, when asked to suffer, whether it be of an organic nature caused by infirmity, whether it be of an emotional and mental nature caused by neurotic and psychotic disorders, or whether it be caused by poverty, loneliness, or cruelty imposed on us, without our having the philosophical means to understand why it is necessary, we may slip into madness or succumb to suicide, murder or other moral disarray for lack of the mental and spiritual support to persevere and take the best advantage of the situation. Reincarnation, therefore, is the light at the end of the tunnel, offering us an honorable exit from the darkness toward the open and clear spaces of life."

The listeners were truly touched by the optimistic narrative permeated with liberating lessons for the conscience, demonstrating that no one can escape either from guilt or from him or herself. By not going into detail about the particular event that had happened in her past life, triggering events in the present, Eneida had prevented insensitive individuals from making inopportune comments about it.

The experience during her partial disengagement in the Sphere of Immortality was identical to that which would later be offered by the venerable Monsignor to the Spanish truculent in Palma de Mallorca after Ramiro's crazed assault.

This was a special night indeed, for the reigning psychosphere invited reflections rich with joy and explosions of happiness.

The participants had not yet recovered from the rapture induced by Eneida, when Father João Pedro asked Dr. Albuquerque for permission to offer some thoughts of his own, if it would not damage the harmony.

After the host and the others encouraged him to proceed, he began:

"Everyone here knows me by the almost apostolic zeal that I hold for the religion I profess and for the conduct I impose on myself. I have sought to be consistent with the priesthood I have embraced ever since my adolescence in the seminary and later on in the relationship with the sheep that the Lord entrusted to me to shepherd. Chastity and celibacy have accompanied my thoughts and attitudes so that I may remain worthy of the ministry I embraced. Nevertheless, as far as the liturgical and dogmatic directives of the Catholic Faith are concerned, I must confess that my mind and sentiments were fraught with conflict and dissatisfaction, leading me to the conclusion of a dramatic new attitude, to which I shall now refer.

"I have always considered God to be the Only, Sovereign and Righteous Father – Omniscient, Omnipresent, Omnipotent... I nourished myself on this natural faith until I reached the age of reason and logic, when I was confronted with questions that did not find convincing answers in the postulates I believed in. Later, studying the history of Christianity and following the footsteps of Jesus, according to the Gospel narratives and the Catholic Church, I found there to be a conflict of information. I concluded that there is the Christianity of Christ and the apostles who accompanied Him, and then there is the Christianity of Rome, according to the imperial and dominant conventions, far removed from the original. I was often caught up in the anguish of such thoughts, considering myself a heretic.

"After hearing many believers' honest confessions about the dramas that assailed them, their difficulties of maintaining sound conduct and doing their best when they were tempted to practice the worst, I wondered at the reasons that produced individuals that are so different from one another. The oneness of life, which I had accepted as real, does not bear up under the analysis presented by the human paradoxes that we all face. In other words, why are geniuses and imbeciles born in the same household? Why are the former created as happy beings and the latter as tormented with no possibility of changing their situation? Why do some suffer right from birth while others are touched by the goddess Fortuna with all the joys and ease imaginable? Why have there been despised races ever since the remote epochs of history, experiencing systematic and ruthless persecutions? How are we to understand the excessive abundance and the devastating misery among individuals, who are all children of the same Father? Why are there premature deaths? Why do good people suffer endlessly while evil ones prosper?... Lastly, there are a thousand questions that cannot be answered by the so-called thesis of *one lifetime*, after which, through death *comes judgment* or *sleep,* until the *Day of the Last Judgment, when the earth will deliver up* all those it had buried... But what about those that had been consumed by flames, devoured by beasts in the wild and fish in the waters, and by drowning? And the victims of the atomic explosions at Hiroshima and Nagasaki?

"But my torments of faith were not reduced to just those conflicts. Could I absolve from all sins those who are perverse criminals, without their having repaired the evils they caused and the destruction of lives they engaged in, only by showing themselves repentant and doing light penance such as saying a few religious prayers and doing a few religious deeds? After death, where would the victims, forsaken by religion, go and where will the criminals themselves go? Is there just one heaven for repentant criminals and untiring strugglers in the faith? Is there one hell for those who committed heinous crimes against humanity, for those who committed adultery, for slanderers, and for those who were responsible for the suffering of thousands of people? Not only that, but what about the liturgies and the sacraments as the only means of salvation... And those who were born in countries and regions where there are no such observances and religious guidelines: how are they to find the Heaven of Eternal Happiness?"

João Pedro looked around and perceived the interest his words were awakening, striking a profound chord with others who were also tormented by such doubts. He paused briefly and then continued:

"The religious and Vatican pomp; the excessive power granted to certain priests who enjoy the exaggerated benefits granted by society; the abusive luxury; the indifference to poverty; the silence before crimes committed by powerful peoples and nations against individuals – none of these find support on any page of the Gospel. On the contrary, they receive severe admonitions. The requirement of chastity and celibacy violates the biological nature of the human being and it exceeds the conditions for a healthy existence, the need for a family and the experience in the home...

"It was then that, hearing about and studying reincarnation in this place, the Gospel, free of the impositions of frustrated theologians and interpreters regarding the beauties of the earth, which made it *a place of exile,* whereas it is actually a blessed paradise – as we see during our times of superior aspirations – I decided to set the cassock aside, break free of the vows and commitments I made to the Catholic Church, and assume the identity of a teacher and an ordinary citizen."

He had had a hunch about the surprise his friends would feel, and indeed they did. So there was another meaningful pause. There was complete silence and one could hear the oppressed breathing of some who attended the meetings, but were still adherents of the Catholic Religion.

Using the expectation that reigned, he continued:

"Some time ago I decided to send documents to Rome requesting my release. It caused a disturbance within my monastery, but fortunately nothing transpired externally. After marches and counter-marches, I have been temporarily relieved of my priestly duties, the administering of the sacraments, the celebration of the Mass and other rites, and I can still either return to the priesthood or leave it for good.

"It gives me great pleasure to announce that I am happy and perfectly free to manage my existence, and to continue teaching as I always have, although I recognize the changes that will take place in my life, the reactions of some well-meaning people and – why not say it? – the persecutions that will be unleashed on me. Nevertheless, the sense of freedom I feel, the joy of having understood and adopted this clear and authentic behavior, without a mask of sanctity or hypocrisy toward my neighbor, conducting myself as I see fit, constitutes a true blessing, which God has given me as a result of the loyalty and honesty with which I have been living.

"So, starting today I will no longer be living at the monastery as an extra citizen in the tormented economy of society, and I hope to contribute to softening its conflicts and disorders, its problems and difficulties."

When he had finished, people were stunned. Some were almost ecstatic; they had not expected the group's studies to have such a profound effect on anyone's behavior.

Dr. Albuquerque realized what was happening amongst his friends and broke the silence. He embraced João Pedro effusively, congratulating him on his decision, and was accompanied by his family and a few friends who had recovered from the shock.

Then, he explained:

"As everybody knows, I, too, went through the same transitions, the same conflicts and difficulties of harmonizing old beliefs with new information, and I opted for the honest and clear conduct that has dignified my existence. I respect the Church and its ministers, its faithful, its purposes, while disagreeing with some of its religious guidelines, which I recognize as necessary for a large part of the individuals who attend it."

And lending more emphasis to his words, he concluded:

"This will always be your home, João Pedro. Its doors are wide open to you to enwrap you in affection and fraternity any moment you need it. And if you find it difficult to continue your function as an educator – for reasons that are not worth examining – until you find something else, there will always be a place for you to earn a living at our metallurgical company. It may be small, but there is room for one more worker."

Eneida, like the others present, was thunderstruck at the news. She immediately remembered their dialogue, when the priest had told her about his deep love for her.

Evangelina served canapés to the friends in celebration of the unexpected event, and then those present gradually bid farewell and left for their own homes.

The impact of the information was too much for some of the former priest's friends. They could not understand the need for such a decision, and thought that he could continue his religious duties while adding the new information and knowledge to his spiritual heritage.

Faint-hearted people always find ways that enable them to keep up the appearance of support for something they actually disagree with; they do not have the courage to take responsibility for what they believe and for what does them good. Thus, they do not feel constrained to make needed changes in behavior, and to endure the struggles that may flow from them. They stick to the conventional, albeit emotionally distant from it.

Men and women of the good are consistent in what they think, in what they say and in what they do. This is the conduct that identifies them as virtuous and honest individuals.

5
LIFE CHARGES EACH ONE ACCORDING TO THE DEBT

Eneida felt that what João Pedro had told everyone was also meant to inform her personally of his recent religious situation and his disagreement with the Church regarding marriage. He had done so with great deft, avoiding addressing the issue of his sentiments and emotions.

Two days after the meeting, which was of great significance to all those in the small Spiritist study group, the ex-priest sought her out. He wanted to talk and could not hide the joy that had come over him because of his new spiritual situation.

He invited her to sit on one of the benches in the flowered yard, where the sunset would become the backdrop for an encounter of love.

She went ahead and sat down, though she was somewhat apprehensive, not knowing what to say to him or what to do.

As soon as they were seated, João Pedro asked her what she thought about the news of his release from his ecclesiastical commitments, whether she had perhaps seen it coming or if she had been completely caught off guard.

Eneida was honest and said that, like all the others who had listened to what he had to say, she had found the news to be pleasantly surprising.

"I thought it was a very happy decision," she told him truthfully. "One cannot feel right by acting in a way that is inconsistent with one's thoughts and emotions, especially when it comes to spiritual issues, because they are so important for a happy existence. My stepfather's decision was exactly the same when he identified with societal life and deep philosophical thought, neither of which was compatible with his religion. Rather than being hypocritical and acting in ways devoid of moral conviction, his decision to pursue different commitments was the best thing he could have done. And everything confirms that fact because it has enabled him to find the happiness he had lacked, both with respect to his sentiments and his social and human accomplishments."

"Well, I'll have to admit that your reflections and the direct way you express your thoughts fascinate me... At the meeting, I felt that it was unnecessary to tell everyone that the sentiments in my heart regarding a future union with you – if the good fates allow it and if it is pleasing to you – were weighing on my conscience, helping me come to a definitive decision."

After a pause, he continued:

"A man is only complete when he meets the woman who is his ideal for sexual communion and the construction of a family. When he's by himself, he's like a bird with a broken wing, unable to soar toward the infinite.

"In your sentiment of affection for me, perhaps there is a great deal of compassion for my pain and solidarity for my suffering. And, for a happy marriage, such would hinder rather than help."

"Yes, in light of the cruel events that have taken place, I have had an aura of tenderness and compassion toward you and the Albuquerques. But that would be the case with any person laden with noble sentiments and worthy to be called a friend. Even so, that has nothing to do with what is dominating me on the inside and is beyond my strength to stifle or renounce. On the other hand, if you were to acquiesce to my wishes, I would not want it to entail any pity... I believe that I am capable of giving you happiness, of helping you forget the past of bitterness and disappointment. Of course I would not try to erase your love for Esperanza from your memory, nor the joyful times you once had, for that would be the ultimate selfishness on my part. My intention is for you and me to be happy also, mutually giving and receiving joy from each other. Otherwise, my sentiments would be unwholesome.

"I deeply regret my current financial situation because, having devoted myself to the Church, I've never had a decent salary – one that would allow me a comfortable life and economic freedom. So I couldn't provide you with the comfort that you enjoy in this home or the one you used to have with your wicked companion. Nevertheless, I would strive to fill the material gap with sentiments of fidelity and love, which no amount of money in the world can buy. And since I'm still young, I would endeavor to struggle hard for everything that can contribute to the happiness of our family... I know that happiness cannot be bought with jewels, which weigh on the body of those who flaunt them, and which can change owners. Happiness can only be purchased with dedication and affection, which enlighten lives – those I can promise to offer you in abundance."

Encouraged by Eneida's silence, as she seemed to be coming back to life from hearing words that had nearly vanished from her memory, he continued:

"I have always wanted to get married and have a family. Often, as I observed the faithful bringing their children to church for worship – the blessed fruit of the union of souls and bodies – I could not help but be somewhat bitter from being unable to procreate. However, I never let myself yearn for cowardly paternity; I mean the kind that results from morally illicit unions between a Catholic priest and a woman who gives in to him, facilitating his emotional balance without receiving his love or public affection in return, but condemned to live in the shadows and be ridiculed by society, which does not excuse her of what it sees as a crime... In this perverse Judeo-Christian society, it is understood that the man has all the rights of freedom, even when he commits the worst indecencies, whereas the woman, as repressed and persecuted today as she was in the past, must shoulder the shame... I always remember Jesus, a paladin of feminism, who was accompanied by women who loved Him and received understanding, affection and dignity from Him. He helped more than a few in deplorable and shameful situations for the time in which they lived, but he also helped others of high social standing, who followed Him and received His unhesitant affection."

He spoke enchantingly, unveiling the noble side of his liberal and human personality, very different from the constraints of his former religion.

"Biblical mercilessness is so strong – cruel, if you will – that when adultery is involved, references are always made to the woman who *sinned,* who was *caught in the act,* the *sinner,* and never to the one to whom she surrendered, who was also caught in the ignoble act of betrayal – the male sinner... Of course, the woman only committed adultery because there was a man who seduced her, who made her fall into the horrible act of disrespecting her husband; but the sociological conventions always hid the presence of the cowardly man who induced her to the crime. But now, that age-old victim of misogyny has found her chance of liberation, her time to demonstrate her greatness."

"You have loads of reason. But I'm afraid that, since woman, generally speaking, is unprepared to live in freedom, she uses it incorrectly and slides into moral license by seeking to imitate that which is most vulgar in man, which is the result of the primeval passions he has not yet corrected. The distance between freedom and debauchery is only a hasty attitude."

"I'm in favor of the notion that when woman is ennobled, she can lift the moral world to a high level of conduct, laying out new pathways of happiness and plenitude for society. For a long time the thinking was that *behind every great man is a great woman,* hiding the prejudice that, still there, puts her on a subaltern plane, when it should be stated that *beside every great man there is a woman of equal moral texture.*"

"In that we are in full agreement, without any mixture of feminism or such."

"And that is how I see you: a great woman, bearer of uncommon values in these tumultuous days. After such a long period of suffering, not a few would have taken another course. They would have given in to rebelliousness or the insane desire for revenge, going down the path of vice and trouble. You are the woman with whom I long to share my dreams, just as I aspire to be part of your aspirations."

"Well, as you can see, all this is very new and strange to me, because I have not allowed myself the dream of a new home."

"But remember that your mother, who also lived through the painful experience of separation, was given a new opportunity and chose Dr. Albuquerque, the great man who became your and Júlio's adoptive father."

"There can be no doubt about that! But my mother's drama aside, my own has had unique, horrendous effects that will last forever."

"*Forever* is a word that should be replaced in your vocabulary with *until the opportune time...* when life absolves you and you begin to smile and dream again."

"I long for that, but I just don't think I deserve it."

"Jesus said, 'Who among you is the one who, if his son asks for bread, will give him a stone, or if he asks for a fish, will give him a serpent?' Much more generous is the Heavenly Father, who always answers according to the request of the child in need. We also learn from Spiritism that, in a correct reference to the Gospel, everything is granted to us according to our works. Moreover, we are not on this earth only to suffer, but to free ourselves from suffering. So, cultivate the hope for better days, trusting in the future and its wonderful gifts. The storm that ravages the landscape also renews it, just as the suffering that lashes the spirit also brings it new perspectives."

As he spoke, the young woman, whose heart was filled with anguish, could not stop the tears that flowed from her eyes.

Driven by the instinct to protect and show immense tenderness, João Pedro gently took her into an accepted embrace. After some years of loneliness and despair, she felt again the warming arms of love enveloping her. She felt comforted; from that moment on she would have someone else to share her anxieties as a woman and her despair as a mother outside the walls of the home where she had always enjoyed protection and refuge. But she remembered that she was not yet divorced, and that made her gently leave his embrace.

Penetrating her with the intuition of affection, João Pedro argued:

"Before God and humans you are free, for you were abandoned and have kept yourself pure. The legalization of your civil divorce is in the works, and then, like me, you will be totally free to make the decision that best suits your female sentiments."

"When that happens, we can discuss this again," she concluded, blushing.

"I beg you, however, to allow me to visit you more often, and not only on the days reserved for our Spiritist meetings."

"Your company is always a great pleasure – it was and always will be. I only ask for time to get used to the new ideas that are replacing those I have cherished over the past few years."

In the distance, Evangelina had been following the conversation of the young couple, although she could not actually hear them, and she was filled with joy. Her motherly intuition slowly but surely hinted that the end of her daughter's trials was approaching. The former priest was a man of excellent moral qualities, industrious and honest, and capable of restoring Eneida to the joy of living, and restarting happy experiences. She withdrew, moved by the idea of seeing them married in the not too distant future.

When Eneida came back into the tastefully decorated living room, she was ready to offer João Pedro some refreshments or coffee. Evangelina took the lead, however, explaining that this was tea-time and inviting him to sit down with both her and Eneida in order to talk for a few minutes before Dr. Albuquerque and Júlio got home from work.

* * *

In his madness, Armando, who had been abandoned by Clara and descended into the haunches of indignity, as already mentioned, used the name of his Rodriguez relatives, some of whom were still residing in V., to surrender to the overflow of the destructive passions.

At the same time, he had gotten in a fight with another of his moral quality, mortally wounding him. The incident caused a huge scandal involving the Rodríguez's, in spite of the fact that his surname was actually Velasquez.

He had been caught red-handed and was thrown in jail without any consideration.

With his binge drinking over, and having recovered something of a conscience, he asked his relatives for help. But they did not give him the least bit of attention and abandoned him to his misery.

Mentally disturbed as a result of his alcoholic extravagances, he became an inconsequential traitor, accusing Manolo and Eneida for his present situation after having thrown Clara and him out of their home, which became a motive for more gossip in the city.

Since every scandal attracts the hunters of human misery, like corpses consumed by microbes, a reporter who was famous for his articles in the "yellow press," those publications which expose people's miseries to the eyes of the public and which thrive in the muck of social inferiority, decided to interview Armando, realizing that he might be able to exploit the situation, causing conflicts and subaltern interests that could be converted into profit and the spread of his reputation.

Armed with police authorization, he was accompanied by a photographer into Armando's cell and recorded statements of the lowest moral quality, which he published in the city's tabloid.

Contained in the sensationalist information – some true, some absurd – were insinuations of how the family's fortune had been acquired, with touches of sarcasm and statements that large sums had been transferred to Spain by sordid means. Manolo, cited several times as an exploiter and drug addict, was labeled a dealer by his insane cousin, and was the main target of the revengeful broadside. Eneida was miraculously spared from the onslaught of perversity and destruction.

The photographs showing the inmate's deplorable condition shocked the community due to the cruelty they portrayed.

For a while, the grandeur and fall of the Rodríguezes simmered in the local talk. The family was shamed by obscene and criminal comments, some of them senseless, demonstrating the informant's imbecility, but never ceasing to be slanderous.

Since the disclosure of secrets involving the depravity of others pleases many human creatures, in spite of their own sordidness, the venal news achieved its purpose, humiliating some honorable individuals and exposing some who were truly despicable.

But over time, things quieted down and Armando died, abandoned in his infested cell, in total mental alienation.

Individuals each choose the earthly trajectory they wish to follow, reaching the goal that has been set.

However, they never lack support and inspiration, which come through various means. Some are subtle; some are direct, but they always lead to ascension and freedom, such that they have no grounds for complaint, nor can they use false allegations to justify their fall when it occurs.

God's love provides for and supplies everything.

* * *

In Palma de Mallorca, events unfolded with a dire outlook.

Little Esperanza looked like a dying plant malnourished by the absence of love, and became seriously ill. Because the organic disturbance, of an emotional origin, was proceeding menacingly, the mother superior at her school informed Manolo, who, in a lamentable state of mind, rushed to visit the little girl.

She had not eaten in days, plunging increasingly into silence and indifference toward everything. This was worrying. When a doctor was asked to examine her, the diagnosis was grim. The child was suffering from profound depression, the causes of which he had not been able to detect. But when he was told that her mother had died under tragic circumstances, the doctor concluded that it was a case of internalization of the conflict, manifesting itself in a disorder of unpredictable consequences. He immediately advised getting help from a psychologist in order to dilute the harmful internal dispositions, encouraging her to rediscover the meaning of life.

Manolo arrived at the school's infirmary and found his daughter prostrate, the odd result of excess therapy and her own unconscious lack of interest toward life.

Seeing her wasted and pale, he was struck with uncontrollable despair. From one aspect, the child was a picture of Eneida's macerated face in the difficult days of his former home. The same curly blond hair, the high forehead, the delicate nose, the high cheekbones, and the full, well-delineated lips were all a clone of the mother. In addition, his guilty conscience from the crime he continued to perpetrate – denying the child the right to be with her mother and maintaining that she had died in a painful situation – assailed him, screaming at him and almost driving him mad.

Now this, added to all the painful experiences he was going through.

In that inner hell, the vigilant, gentle nun suggested that the girl be sent home to be with her family. She would experience a change of emotional climate and could perhaps recover more easily. Neither keeping her at the school nor putting her in a hospital would offer her the benefit of domestic warmth.

The home is always a sanctuary of love that vitalizes beings, especially if it is built on ethical-moral values conducive to harmony and well-being.

Olga felt that she was Esperanza's spiritual mother, but the girl had not had the opportunity to experience her presence, due to the imbalance of her husband, who had chosen to enroll her in the school without telling Olga the truth about the vicissitudes the girl had experienced, which he himself had caused. Olga was ready to welcome her and to assist her with maternal devotion.

Somehow, her motherly instincts found a happy opportunity to manifest, despite the distressing circumstances of the moment.

After the family had made the necessary arrangements, retaining the same physician and psychologist, the little jewel was taken to the luxury apartment, though not like on other occasions such as on fun-filled weekends, but to await the great decision of Life.

Weak and glum, Esperanza had been lovingly accommodated in a comfortable room, assisted by the doctor and competent nurses. Several days passed without the debility improving, despite the nourishment provided by Olga, who displayed a lofty expression of noble sentiments, inspired by her tutelary spirit. In a wan voice, while her sincerely emotional father gazed at her in tears, Esperanza said in her childish language:

"Yesterday I dreamed that a very beautiful lady came to fetch me in order to take me to my mother."

Her clear eyes were filled with tears as she continued the narration:

"She told me that my mother is still alive, that she did not die, as I was told."

Taken with astonishment, Manolo screamed and felt like running to the balcony to throw himself off and fall flat on the stone sidewalk a few stories down. Frenzied, he went on the attack instead:

"That's a lie! She did too die. I saw her stretched out on the ground, dead, the poor thing."

Olga tried to calm him down with encouraging words while showing interest in the information provided by the obviously illuminated girl.

Esperanza continued:

"She was very beautiful, and was dressed in flowing white fabric. Her face glowed as if there was a light burning inside her. She smiled, stretched out her arms toward me, and spoke as if she was singing a sweet melody: 'Your suffering is about to end. The dark night in which you have been looking for your mother will turn into a dawn of joy. Somewhere she is waiting for you and will receive you with infinite love. I will come and get you soon so that you will not have to suffer any more. Your tears will dry up, and the song of love that your mother always used to sing before you fell asleep will be repeated in your ears.'"

The girl made a great effort to babble the words, overcome by growing emotion.

Manolo was terrified and did not know what to say or even what to think.

The court of Truth was showing him how no one can escape its directives, nor can they erase or destroy them in the course of days.

Olga took the child's icy cold hands and, trying to warm them with her own, enfolding her in sweetness, spoke to her tenderly:

"If you'd like, I'll sing to you like your mother used to. I don't know what the song was, but I know a lot of other lullabies that help little children get to sleep. Why haven't you ever told me this or asked me to do it?"

The sweet woman was almost overcome with emotion. She had discovered the greatness of maternal love and inwardly regretted not yet having been honored with the happiness of procreation, even though she might have experienced such joy by enfolding another mother's child in her arms.

Just then, Little Esperanza looked at her astonished father and confessed to him in an unforgettable manner:

"I'm scared, Daddy! It's like I'm crossing a really high bridge and I'm afraid I'll fall off. Help me, Daddy!"

Manolo could not contain himself and began to blaspheme, contorted from the pain of a guilty conscience.

Olga tried to calm him down, telling him that this was too serious of a time for him to let himself be imbalanced.

"Can't you see that your daughter's dying?" she cried. "Call the doctor and tell him it's an emergency."

Panic set in. Servants rushed about at their master's cries, and one of them, groaning in anguish and pain, called an ambulance.

The girl's face was discolored and she was in a cold sweat. Her eyes glistened and her chest was heaving.

"Do you love your mommy very much?" Olga asked, not fearing to evoke the *deceased,* as had been forbidden by her demented companion. It did not matter to her at the moment.

A very sad smile was drawn on the face of the dying child, who replied:

"My mommy is like an angel, and if she's dead, she's surely waiting for me in heaven. But the lady who visited me said she's alive."

"She was right, because no one really dies. The person loses the body, but the spirit continues to live. That's what she meant, don't you think?"

There was no response. Esperanza's eyes closed for a few seconds as thick tears streamed down. Her breathing was short and labored. One could see the unbalanced beating of her heart.

Olga asked someone to call the priest and the Mother Superior of the school where the child had spent those bitter years of her brief existence.

She ordered candles to be lit and rushed to grab her rosary in order to pray according to the religious tradition of her faith.

The minutes dragged by. The individuals who had been called were trickling in. The doctor was truly sorry to report that the girl's heart had lost its rhythm and, although he injected her with a stimulant, he stated that the end was near. The Mother Superior had also arrived accompanied by one of the teachers and, kneeling beside the bed, tried to encourage the little girl to advance in the direction of Life, trusting in God.

The silence, broken by sobs in the large room, was immersed in the panting breath of the fragile existence draining away at the impact of death.

Esperanza suddenly opened her eyes and smiled, announcing:

"The lady... has come... to get me... She's smiling... and is calling me... saying... I don't… have to be… afraid."

She tried to raise her fragile body as if she wished to sit up, and stretched out her arms toward where she said the noble spirit was. Then she fell back upon the soft cushions and breathed her last.

Manolo was overcome with grief, as he was totally unprepared for reality. He tried to tear out his hair and he beat his head against the walls and doors, before being subdued by the servants and the doctor, who injected him with a sedative.

Olga, displaying great poise, counseled with the Mother Superior about the steps to be taken. Meanwhile, the doctor signed the death certificate and sent for the representative of a well-known, upscale funeral parlor so that arrangements could be made for the wake and the burial.

The body was moved to the chapel for the wake. Family members were quickly summoned, and the news was spread, arriving, via telephone, in the town of V., South Africa.

The Albuquerque received the heartbreaking news, and the affliction stabbed them most painfully. Eneida fainted and medical attention was immediately requested, taking into account her organic fragility, while the mantle of suffering cloaked already embittered hearts.

The family was unanimous in agreeing that Divine Providence was closing part of the history of their lives with a very distressing chapter but one that would end the drama they had been going through.

The tragedy of the little bird stolen from the nest had now ended, and she was soaring in the direction of Infinity for a definitive reunion at a later time.

The Albuquerques knew that Little Esperanza had died evoking her mommy and remembering her lullabies. It was an extraordinary comfort to all, confirming that evil is transitory and that no one can silence the voice of truth, which always rises to reign.

The emptiness left by the feeble little flower of flesh would remain unfilled, waiting for the happy moment when she would return to her mother's arms.

Olga and her stunned husband went to the chapel at the cemetery where the body awaited interment.

The following day, a mass was held before the burial of the physical remains.

The funeral rites were carefully organized. Children from the school participated in the liturgy, singing especially the *Agnus Dei,* which had a powerful impact, as if they were veritable angels singing a song in homage to the beloved deceased...

The gloomy decor, the somewhat macabre rite, and the words uttered by the priest, loaded with mourning and pain, were the backdrop presented by a religious belief that advocates life and honors death with all the black paint of annihilation.

When the burial ceremony ended, the guests dispersed and the couple returned home, now marked by Little Esperanza's final moments. Manolo plunged into the darkness of madness.

Sleep, which was already a problem because of interference by his discarnate enemies, became even more troubled.

Rejoicing due to the tragic events that brought the bitter pain to their enemy, the Portuguese and N'Bondo intensified their siege, preparing to consummate their plan to put an end to his life.

In the days that followed, Manolo slipped into dementia. He had loved his daughter very much in his own, peculiar, sickly way. Her loss and his guilt wounded him profoundly, with no chance for a quick recovery.

Olga arranged for a psychiatrist, and admission to a clinic for sleep therapy was seen as the best solution, considering the severity of his disorder and constant suicidal impulses.

The terrible news was made public with spicy comments among Manolo's friends, fellow stock investors, and members of his social club.

In their foolishness, human beings disregard solidarity during delicate moments in other people's lives. They do not realize that pain is common to all, and all are visited by it at the opportune moment. Unpopular to some individuals because of his presumptuous and ostentatious temperament, and well-received by others, Manolo had not been able to form a circle of close friends. In fact, the number of real friends in the different segments of society is always reduced. As long as life flows abundantly and one's prominence is in society's high circles of futility, or power stokes one's vanity, one is surrounded by coryphaei and flatterers. Soon, however, the winds blow from the other direction and loneliness becomes the partner of the abandoned.

On the one hand, Manolo's sleep therapy harmonized his brain's neurons, helping to stabilize its synapses, but on the other hand, it left him entirely at the mercy of his discarnate foes, who hounded him during his spirit's partial disengagement due to his spirit's state of torpor. Undoubtedly, besides intervening in his somatic body, the medications were absorbed by the *subtle envelope of the soul*[14] and anesthetized it also to some degree, impeding its clear reasoning and ideal movement while freed from its carnal bonds.

Finding themselves completely free to act and trouble their enemy, the discarnates did not spare him from name-calling and recriminations, accusing him of being responsible for Esperanza's death, stoking his guilt regarding the lie about Eneida's life in order to make his guilty conscience throw him into complete disorder.

Thus, during the times when his physical body seemed to be asleep, he was actually being tormented and persecuted, suffering the tortures of Tantalus.[15]

The days that followed were meant to adapt the people that surrounded him to the new demands of the existential process.

---

14 Perispirit – Tr.

15 Tantalus - mythological King of Lydia who, after stealing the delicacies of the gods, handed them over to human beings. In disgust, the gods drove him into Tartarus, a place with a lake and many trees laden with fruit. He was unable to reach any of it, however, and was overcome by perpetual hunger and thirst (note of the spirit author).

Olga proved to be an excellent wife and skillful investor in her husband's stead, directing the application of the assets and stocks owned by both, according to the advice of ethical brokers.

Manolo was now at home while continuing his psychiatric treatment. Hence he was incapable of assuming the responsibilities relevant to his business.

With the documents and keys to the couple's property – guided by her husband, who at times temporarily regained his lucidity, albeit with difficulty – Olga was at the office one day and remembered the diamond necklace and earrings. She decided to have a look at them. Manolo had told her that he kept them in the office safe to keep them from being stolen at home by one of the servants.

With some care, she managed to wrest the combination to the safe from him, on the grounds that she needed to check some deeds and documents. She took out the costly case and its contents and, closing the door and windows, paused to examine the fabulous stones.

They did belong to her, after all, and she had had the opportunity to wear them on their wedding day.

She was impressed with the brilliance and coldness of the gemstones, characteristic of their reality as just stones, their worth attributed to them by human greed and cunning, being only less common...

She put the necklace on first and then the other pieces. Taken with a peculiar emotion, the kind that stems from the ambition for earthly treasures, she approached the mirror and looked at herself.

She felt like a powerful goddess. The sparkle of the set due to the slightest movement gave her a special beauty, much to the liking of female vanity.

Sighing and almost trembling, she grasped the main stone of the necklace, closed her eyes and said to herself: "They're mine, and I will do whatever it takes to keep them."

She had no idea what she was saying...

After that day, she would open the safe now and then and delight herself with precious set.

Nevertheless, the successful investor avoided telling her still shaken husband about the satisfaction she felt when she held the necklace in her hands and wore it around her neck, even if it was only in the silence and solitude of the office. She was afraid he would react and stop her from doing so again.

* * *

Ramiro Alvarez was thrilled when he learned of the tragedies that had hit the Rodríguez family.

He had survived his pervious encounter with Manolo and had had enough time to reflect. He was resentful and hateful, and he swore that he would never give up his ambition to possess the diamonds – he would find a way. The extraordinary sight of the sparkling gems on that sunny afternoon had never faded from his memory. It was as if he had been hypnotized by the glitter of the stones and by the composition of the necklace and other pieces.

Knowing that their owner was ruined and under vigorous therapy, he rejoiced at the possibility of dealing with a demented man in the future instead of a shrewd, quick foe.

As soon as he learned of Manolo's return home for an extended convalescence, he had the audacity to send him a bouquet of roses accompanied with a card, on which he expressed his greetings and hopes for a quick recovery.

Olga did not know who Ramiro was when she received the flowers, but when she told Manolo, he was struck by a fit of hatred. His eyes opened wide, and he had her toss the roses into the trash can because they were from a crook, an avowed foe. He was trembling and began uttering disjointed words.

The flowers were thrown out and they were not mentioned again.

The criminal's audacity had no measure. Using a mutual friend, who had gone to visit Manolo, he asked him to intervene and ask Manolo to please forgive him, for he was deeply sorry for their incident earlier, which he intended to make up for through sincere friendship.

The attempt failed, however, because whenever Manolo even heard the name of the hated accomplice, he would become exasperated and aggressive. He was also inimical toward anyone attempting to be an intermediary for a rapprochement, which he said would be impossible.

Let us acknowledge the fact that, in addition to being contemptible, Manolo was also spiteful and hateful, as is often the case with all those who tread the ways of cunning and crime.

6
NEW EXPERIENCES: SOME GRATIFYING, OTHERS PAINFUL

João Pedro's constant pursuit of Eneida ended up finding a home in her embittered heart. One year after Esperanza's passing, she communicated at one of the family meetings through Evangelina. Eneida's heart was reinvigorated and she resolved to live again so that she could contribute in some way to a happier society in the future.

Meanwhile, her divorce was granted, thanks to the fact that she had been abandoned by her husband, who had fled the country and had never given any explanation for it, in addition to having kidnapped their daughter, whom the authorities had not been able to extradite – a seeming legal absurdity. However, as is still the case nowadays, there was a period of paradoxes in the different segments of society, including the Judiciary, which often carries out justice in various areas after receiving a substantial bribe. Ironically, that is why the goddess Justice is portrayed wearing a blindfold...

The political-social situation in South Africa had become almost unbearable: crimes were committed at any time of the day and night, the number of robberies was shameful, and the police were unable to maintain order. In fact, the police themselves were targets of perverse attacks on the part of fanatics, who inflicted awful revenge on their former employers, thus committing the same unbearable crime against humanity.

The discrimination by Whites against Blacks is truly ignoble, but revenge carried out by vengeful Blacks against Whites is no less shameful.

Skin color does not characterize the moral reserves of individuals. There are dignified, selfless, worthy and wise, cruel, primitive, and insensitive men and women in all races and skin colors. The spirit indwelling the body is what externalizes its stage of evolution in the flesh in which it lives and moves in the physical world.

Supporting or encouraging any kind of retaliation on the part of former victims of racial discrimination means returning to the stage of barbarism and primitivism rather than superseding it.

The spirit is destined for the stars, and keeping it stuck in the mire of the vile passions is unfortunate behavior that only retards its moral progress.

Whenever the victims of any distressing circumstance attain new-found freedom to which they are not accustomed, they almost always lapse into abusing it, and are sometimes encouraged to seek revenge, committing the same heinous acts that they themselves used to condemn for afflicting them in the *flesh of the soul.*

Love, forgiveness, compassion and charity are always the wonderful titles of ennoblement that dignify human creatures in whatever situations they find themselves, especially when following the pathway of happiness.

The Albuquerques were experiencing one of the best periods of their existence after having overcome the anguish imposed by their psychopathic relative. Now free from the disgrace he had inflicted on them with such precision, they won the respect and solidarity of the community's illustrious individuals and many of the unfortunate ones who were benefited by them. Their metallurgical business had grown considerably, giving Dr. Albuquerque and the industrious Júlio highly successful financial results. Their mansion stood out in the community due to its majesty, its immense yards, its well-treated and kindly household staff, and lastly, by the guests who frequented it.

Moreover, the Spiritist meetings continued to be held in a specially constructed room outside the residence. The weekly study groups attracted the city's scholars and intellectuals who were interested in learning about the Spiritist postulates. Many of them also appreciated the honest discussions with their socially and culturally refined host.

There were also days dedicated exclusively to mediumship activities, involving only those members who displayed knowledge of the Spiritist Doctrine, especially novice mediums who worked under Evangelina, whose sensitivity provided high-level spirit communications.

In this climate of all kinds of achievements, João Pedro's courtship of Eneida received sympathy from her family, especially Júlio – who felt highly attached to the former Catholic priest – as well as friends who foresaw a future rich in blessings.

João Pedro was an admirable educator who had had no difficulty in continuing to give public and private lessons, especially in languages such as English, French, and Latin, in which he was well-versed, as well as in mathematics and physics. Initially, as he began laying out his course for the future, he had worked in the office of Dr. Albuquerque's company, but he knew that he was born to teach – it fascinated him and enriched him with joy.

The wedding was scheduled for approximately one month after the first anniversary of Esperanza's discarnation. Eneida and Evangelina used all the time available for making the bridal outfit and organizing the new residence where the bride and groom were to live. It was a wedding gift to them from all the Albuquerques...

At first João Pedro insisted on declining the generous offer, explaining that he himself wanted to procure their residence – preferably a modest, comfortable rental, while he worked to afford the home that he desired mentally and emotionally.

But Dr. Albuquerque convinced him to acquiescence, explaining:

"Eneida is our de facto and direct heir. Everything that we as her family own is hers. Would it be fair of us to let her enjoy the possessions that are already hers only after our death? Instead of later, why not give them to her now so that all of us can enjoy the pleasure of the gift? Júlio is still single, and he regards his sister as a true cherub, whom he loves and for whom he struggles. He especially insists on giving a home to his beloved sister and future brother-in-law, whom he greatly respects and esteems. The rest of us agree completely."

"I'm afraid you'll think that, because of my economic need, I'm interested in your family's assets, and not in my love for the one whom I've chosen."

"Well, my friend," Dr. Albuquerque concluded, "people talk about everything, each person according to his or her own ability to feel and to understand, which is perfectly natural. You're young and you're a fighter capable of making superlative sacrifices, and the future will bless you with the crown of victory. The important thing is your love for each other, which will enable you both to plan and concretize a future of deserved harmony and happiness. So don't be embarrassed and accept our gift. It is dedicated to you too.

Taken with sincere emotion, João Pedro agreed to the offer.

The wedding invitations were sent to those in the circle of friendship. Excluded were any relatives of Manolo who occasionally maintained a discreet social relationship with Evangelina, who put herself emotionally above the unfortunate occurrences, never referring to them, nor their cause.

By reason of modesty and honesty, both Evangelina and Eneida were willing to maintain an attitude of discretion towards the Rodríguez clan. Since the two had never bothered any of its members by accusing them, blaming them or seeking information from them that they did not spontaneously grant – although some of them were aware of all the intrigues and subterfuges of Manolo's crime – now was not the time to re-establish stronger ties of communication and relations.

Prudence is always an attitude of wisdom in the behavior of human beings, and must always be preserved.

The longed-for day arrived. The family-court judge was asked to perform the civil ceremony at the Albuquerque residence, decorated with caprice and very good taste.

A red carpet stretched from the entryway to the hall, which was ornamented by two columns of white marble. The hall led to a small room where the wedding ceremony would take place.

In the back yard, a number of colored canvas canopies created a well-arranged environment where deft waiters served drinks and canapés – there were no alcoholic drinks because of the family's Spiritist beliefs and the groom's moderate habits. The guests gathered under the canopies around small tables covered with white, intricately embroidered linen tablecloths and decorated with orchids and protea – the national flower – tied with colored silk ribbons, providing just the right accent.

Sèvres porcelain, paired with Bohemian crystal, was set next to the silverware, and silver napkin rings held the linen serviettes, which matched the tablecloth, constituting harmonious dinner sets. The dinner service was specially ordered for the guests from a famous local buffet.

Everything exuded good taste and refinement, without the typical extravagances in the homes of the nouveaux riches.

The huge wedding cake lay on a special table in the middle of the yard for the culminating moment.

Four five-year-olds – two ring bearers and two flower girls – dressed for the occasion, carrying the wedding rings and delicate bouquets of forget-me-nots, welcomed the bride and groom and stood by their side as the marriage celebration unfolded, marked by conventional formalism but enriched by the judge – a committed Spiritist – who proffered praiseworthy advice to the couple, commenting on the meaning of marriage for Christian people who embraced the Spiritist Revelation.

Then the newly-weds went to the central table for Eneida to toss the delicate bouquet of orchids she had been carrying to complement her beige outfit, which emphasized her harmonious shape. On her short well-combed hair she wore a small Panama hat that matched her suit and shoes, and with its white tulle band it gave her a touch of noble maturity compatible with her existence.

The groom was dressed in a gray pin-stripe suit, complete with silk waistcoat over a white shirt and bow tie, emphasizing his slender figure and the happiness displayed on his honest face in a permanent smile.

When Eneida tossed the bouquet over her shoulders, it was caught by one of her young friends, who was exultant, exclaiming:

"Well, I've got the flowers and now all I need is a groom. But for me that seems to be the most important and hardest part."

There was hearty, spontaneous laughter from everyone in response to the lucky girl's natural confession.

The newlyweds were congratulated by their relatives first, and then by the guests, who were standing in a noisome and cheerful line.

A string ensemble, specially hired to embellish the party, began playing beautiful songs, and joy filled everyone's heart.

At 9:00 p.m. a magnificent dinner was served. It was very well accepted and highly appreciated for the quality of the dishes. In addition to the local delicacies of the English tradition, there were specialties of the French cuisine, highly desirable by any gourmet. Some lamented the absence of quality wines, hard liquor and digestives... But they contented themselves with what was served and they respected their hosts' decision.

At 11:00 p.m. the newlyweds said goodbye to the guests and drove to their own home, without the usual honeymoon escape... Mature and aware of the responsibility they had assumed, they would strive to stay balanced at all times so that nothing strange or unusual would draw attention to their behavior.

All the guests eventually left for their homes, extolling the Albuquerques' generosity and facing their own worries and anxieties.

In the days immediately following, the social columns in the newspapers referred to the solemnities of the marriage, thus bringing to an end the string of sufferings that had marked the family's existence.

* * *

Nevertheless, the twists and turns of fate brought back to the city someone who had fled from there with a significant amount of money after the death of the Portuguese. It was Mayuso, the former employee at the metallurgical company, whom Manolo had used to execute the loan shark, and who, after the crime and on the advice of his employer, had escaped with his family to the province of Natal, whence he had come.

He had gone back to Vryheid, a rich coal-mining region, where he tried to find a place to live a financially worry-free existence. The reward for the crime, offered to him by the one who had engendered it, would be enough to enable him to live a relatively quiet life while pursuing some gainful activity. This was necessary in order to avoid attracting the attention of his fellow countrymen, who writhed in the clutches of indigence. At first the criminal was able to remain discreet, stating that he had had to return to his origins in order to begin a new life. But he had found it difficult to find paid work that would support him and his family, so he had begun to spend the reward money, using alcohol and getting lost in boasting, attaching to himself importance that he did not deserve, since the most significant thing he had ever been capable of was the treacherous, cowardly murder of the Portuguese.

Without any moral structure, despite the fragile values he had displayed on the occasion of his daughter's illness prior to his escape, Manolo's help and contribution as co-author of the murder, he soon fell to degradation, joining others like himself to commit assaults and brazen robberies, taking advantage of the prevailing disorder in the country. A repeat offender, he would be thrown in jail and then released, only to end up back there, where he suffered cruel punishment at the hands of the police, erasing what remained of his dignity.

Staying true to his commitment not to reveal the crime, he imposed on himself the duty to face even death in unyielding silence. However, as he lost his self-respect and was finally driven to economic misery, because his resources had dwindled over the years, he repeatedly remembered the Boss.

His bad tendencies emerged, inspiring him to seek more resources from the one person who could offer them, since it was for him that he had committed the vile and irrecoverable act in the first place.

When difficulties and illnesses became too much for him, it occurred to him to return to V. to beseech help and protection from the one who had caused his misery. He said to himself: Why should I suffer misery, hunger and sickness while my rich Boss enjoys pleasure and greatness, despite having been the mastermind of the murder? Is a destroyed life worth only the amount I received?

Thus, equally inspired by the forces of evil, who collude with those who are similar to them, he decided to travel in search of that which he believed he deserved in order to recover and support his disordered family.

Consequently, he sought out the metallurgical company and presented himself to Júlio, whom he had known slightly before he had become a partner of the company.

"I have to talk to the Boss right this minute," he said, pretending to be embarrassed.

He was completely unaware of all that had happened after his shameful flight.

Júlio explained that he was now one of the owners and was at his disposal.

Awkwardly, Mayuso explained that he needed to talk to *Doctor* Manuel Rodríguez, the C.E.O. and owner of the place.

Júlio explained that Manolo had sold the company to him and Dr. Albuquerque several years ago.

"So where can I find my old boss? I have urgent business to discuss with him."

"We have no idea where he is. No one but his family can help you."

On his face hardened by the ignoble acts he had committed, Mayuso expressed all the disappointment that invaded him. He asked once more:

"Isn't there any way I can talk to the boss? I worked for him for many years before going back to the province of Natal. I need his help right now."

"Unfortunately," said Júlio, somewhat dismayed, "I cannot help you. I'm very sorry."

Having lost the blow he intended to apply, the unscrupulous criminal attempted to arouse Júlio's curiosity, speaking reticently:

"It's just that... he owes me a debt... because of a job... I did for him... and I did it exactly the way he wanted... so that today... he can live happily."

"Even so, there's nothing I can do."

Júlio picked up on the morbid psychosphere around Mayuso and decided not to meddle.

And because Mayuso insisted almost audaciously on help in finding Manolo, he was escorted out without further ado.

But first, furious at having grasped the fact that he had been used and then discarded as disposable and useless, whereas the real criminal, the one who had engendered the murder had gotten away, remaining unreachable by justice, Mayuso whispered between clenched teeth:

"This isn't how it's going to be. He's going to pay me one way or another."

Mayuso was very familiar with the city and the miserable neighborhood where he used to live. He managed to hide out in the hut of another wretch while he worked out a plan to get more money or to get revenge on the one who had made him miserable, even though he had rewarded him with the gold of shame.

When Júlio arrived home, he told his stepfather and mother what had happened, adding that there was some mystery in Mayuso's relationship with Manolo.

"I wonder if that was one of the reasons why Manolo took off like he did," replied Dr. Albuquerque.

The matter was dropped after a few quick comments, however.

In the days that followed, Mayuso tried unsuccessfully to approach Manolo's relatives.

He then got the idea to look up Gumercinda, the Portuguese's widow. She would certainly be interested in finding out what had actually happened to her husband.

With perverse stubbornness, he tracked her down and showed up at her office. As already stated, she had remarried and had taken over the management of her ex's racket.

Informed by a secretary that a Black urgently wanted to speak to her, Gumercinda had him disrespectfully escorted out, saying that she did not have time to waste on despicable people.

Of course, she was in a socially and economically enviable situation, enjoying the spoils of the Portuguese's unbridled greed, as well as the shameful exploitation of her clients, extorted by her own extreme avarice.

Despised and emotionally imbalanced, the vile and unstructured man realized that this would be his last chance to get some easy money. He was afraid to go to the police because they would imprison him for life, since his former boss, now an international fugitive, could not be apprehended, much less be incriminated, for lack of evidence. After all, he was only the mastermind of the tragedy; not the executor. And between the two, it was obvious that the white man would be acquitted if he were to be put on trial; but not Mayuso, who would possibly receive the "reward" of being hanged in Pretoria...

Feeling frustrated and lost, he got drunk in the ghetto where he was living and, troubled as he was, he got in a brawl with another trouble-maker, who stabbed him to death...

* * *

The teaching of Jesus always has its place at any time and under any circumstance, inviting deep reflections, as when he was being taken prisoner in the Garden of Olives, and Peter, in despair, took the sword of one of the soldiers and, in His defense, cut off the ear of the high priest's servant. With great serenity, after healing the wound, the Excellent Friend said to his careless disciple: "Put your sword in its place, for all who draw the sword will die by the sword."

There is no irreversible fatalism involved, but one unresolved crime does lead to another and its mark only disappears after it has been atoned for.

Reincarnation is the instrument granted by God to provide this providential therapy to all offenders. However, it will not always have to occur via the same means that generated the crime; other mechanisms may be used, especially love. Nonetheless, the most common means is for the victims, feeling that they are creditors of justice, to duplicate the wrong that had been done to them, demanding payment be made in the same manner – or for the Sovereign Laws to arrange an equivalent situation.

The fact is that no one can leave the debt unpaid *sine die* – it will inevitably be regularized.

Mayuso had been drawn by the predominance of the Law of Cause and Effect to return to the site of the murder, where he became a victim of his own criminal impulsivity.

* * *

Meanwhile, in Magaluf, Manolo was delirious. He had not recovered the mental serenity necessary to manage his properties. Even under strong medication, he was still semi-deranged, either due to the degeneration of neurons because of alcoholism, or the pernicious influence of the two discarnate enemies who gave him no respite.

He had lost an enormous amount of weight due to the difficulty of nourishing himself as necessary, for many times before a meal he would be overwhelmed with despair and hallucinations, resulting in repeated nervous crises.

He was given special care by his loving wife and by specially hired health-care givers who monitored him twenty-four hours a day, following the psychiatrist's orders.

Consequently, alienated from reality, he was completely unaware of events that affected his existence.

In this state of affairs, one year elapsed after Esperanza's death. Manolo showed slight improvement, even though the obsessive persecution had lessened. He accompanied Olga to the office now and then to try to return to the reality of the business.

One day while concentrating in the work room, he recalled the scuffle with Ramiro and automatically remembered the diamond necklace and earrings.

Unaware of the fact that Olga was also in love with the set, he asked her to leave the room so that he could open the safe alone... She decided to inform him that she had already found the safe with the fabulous set and had examined it more than once.

He almost lost control, but quickly understood that her discovery of the case and its priceless contents was bound to happen, considering the fact that, for several months, she had taken care of all the accounts, the notes and the documents kept in the safe.

As partners of the same interest, she asked his permission to remove the jewelry from the safe, after having closed the doors and windows and having lowered the curtains to avoid being seen by some curious person, or by someone walking in on them and seeing the dazzling necklace.

Olga took the jewelry box wrapped in navy-blue out of the safe and opened it.

Manolo could not contain the exclamation of jubilation and wonder that always flowed from his lips whenever he saw the fascinating sight of the glittering gems.

He lifted the necklace with both hands and, a bit weak-kneed, he approached Olga and put it around her white neck.

Automatically she took the earrings and put them on. She was flushed with emotion and looked resplendent.

She brought her hands to her chest and said:

"They're so beautiful! With their brilliance and stone-cold silence, these jewels are certainly worth a few lives."

Manolo went pale as death at his wife's statement and stammered enigmatically:

"Yes!... Worth... a few... lives!"

The automatism of reminiscences instantly took him back to distant times, when, loving his first wife, he dreamed of adorning her with the necklace, although he also wanted to acquire something valuable that would be easy to move; something that could be taken out of the country without major problems. He had always cherished the desire to move from South Africa to Europe, where he hoped to receive better blessings from the goddess Fortuna... And for that to become a reality, he would have to accumulate assets abroad that would enable him to realize his dreams.

During that moment of recollection, he realized that he had always been emotionally unstable; nevertheless he had acquired the precious set through commitments that were far beyond his ability to regularize – such had been the amounts he had borrowed for his fabulous purchase.

That was what had deluded him, pushing him to commit murder, though he had not done so with his own hands; still, he was its intellectual author and channel of the resources for its execution.

He began to tremble, weakened as he still was, turned deathly pale and began to sweat profusely. But Olga, dazzled by the beautiful set that held her mesmerized as she gazed at herself in the mirror, did not even notice the conflict that had taken control of her husband.

He then relived the events of Eneida's abandonment, hoping she would get murdered by some wretch on that deserted road; the abduction of Esperanza; his new marriage; the girl's mysterious illness; her untimely death...

He burst into mournful sobbing, startling Olga and bringing her back to reality. She was shocked by Manolo's appearance, disfigured and paralyzed with pain.

She rushed to the safe, deposited the case inside, and quickly closed it, and, because her husband's state had worsened, she called an office assistant. Manolo began to struggle, victimized by a terrible psychotic crisis that caused a mental breakdown.

The doctor was called, who requested an ambulance to transfer the patient to the psychiatric clinic, where he would remain indefinitely.

Let us say that, finally, Manuel Rodríguez, the tormented Manolo, was hopelessly insane.

In his deliria, he would fight with the discarnate enemies, who stigmatized him, playing on his guilty conscience and using his perversity to exact payment, which, in their own delusion, they took upon themselves, far removed from the Sovereign Laws of God and His Justice.

Manolo would never recover and passed down the dark corridor of despair to total dementia.

7
DIAMONDS
THAT DELUDE

The days that followed were painful, dark for Olga after the fearsome diagnosis, although it had, more or less, been expected. It was highly unlikely that Manolo would ever recover. At one moment he would appear to be hebetated, far-removed from reality; the next moment he would be in a frenzy of excitement. His lack of appetite and the strong medication debilitated him even further. He had aged visibly and showed no identifiable signs of the former, ambitious, talkative, attention-seeking, arrogant businessman.

Over time, advised by her lawyers, as legal heir to the couple's assets, she decided to sell the brokerage office connected with the Palma de Mallorca Stock Exchange, and began living on the enormous income, which would provide her with an opulent existence – especially since there were no descendants. She displayed a healthy and superior character, compared to the near-indifference of Manolo's parents toward him. They had become aware of his tragic circumstances only by the string of events that culminated in the cruel breakdown, and had offered nothing more than empty words, one or two quick visits of feigned sympathy, and nothing more.

Selfishness is a cancer that devours the human creature and poisons souls in regard to their neighbor and the society in which they live.

Selfish individuals live by the popular expression: *Today for me, tomorrow for you.* They forget everything that wisdom teaches, though it is rich in the precious essence that has flowed from human experience down through the ages.

But who are those who can be considered self-sufficient to the point of not needing anyone else, even if they possess the most enviable monetary resources? They will always have to resort to someone, paid or not, in order to advance along the narrow corridor of suffering, which exempts no one on their inexorable journey that answers for the moral and spiritual purification of all.

We can safely state that the Rodríguezes were made of the cold marble of indifference when it came to affectivity, even in relation to their own family members.

The way they had contributed to Eneida and Esperanza's unhappiness by approving of and supporting their son's sordid plot reflected their level of sentiment.

Feigning love toward Manolo, they actually harbored bitter resentment toward him because they felt they had been robbed of the assets they had left in his care in Africa. And this was a good time for them to feel life's vengeance, for its dagger may take a long time to finally descend on offenders, reaping their existence, but it never fails to execute the final blow that is destined for them...

The Rodríguezes recognized the spendthrift's unfortunate demeanor and extravagances, a fact that pushed them away affectively, which they justified amongst themselves in their intimate conversations.

It was a case affirming: *Like son, like parents!*

Olga assumed the responsibility of supporting him and she remained faithful to him, in spite of the ambitious and unscrupulous suitors who tried to woo her with their eyes on her assets.

Psychologically matured by the occurrences, and somewhat bitter for not having been a biological mother, she had truly loved Esperanza, whom Manolo had banished to the school. She had had the girl in her home for a short time, and even though it was already quite late in her life, she had had the wonderful chance for her motherly instincts to be touched very deeply.

Meanwhile, in the city of V., in Africa, the news of Manolo's plunge into the dark ocean of madness astonished some people, but not the Albuquerques. They knew his venal character, as well as the inexorability of the Universal Laws, which always reach those who violate them – not always immediately, but surely, making them responsible and calling them to re-establish the equilibrium that must reign everywhere.

Eneida was also notified of the tragic event. She truly felt sorry for Manolo, because, in spite of the dreadful pain and suffering he had inflicted on her, almost leading her to insanity or suicide – from which she had been rescued by the religious faith that had soothed her sentiments – as time passed she began to nourish a special form of compassion for him. Later, when she had found out about Esperanza's discarnation, resentment wanted to dominate her, but once more she had overcome it with relative peace-of-mind by trusting in God and His love.

As heavenly compensation, she had found true love. It lacked any sense of childish rapture, but was imbued with sure and noble affection for the man who now filled the aching or empty emotional spaces that the cruelty of her insane ex had caused her.

At the first opportunity, when the family got together for the Gospel in the Home – we will remember that it was a weekly event, endowed with a sense of forgiveness and Christian solidarity – Dr. Albuquerque offered beautiful intercessory vibrations on behalf of his former son-in-law, praying fervently for his almost impossible restoration.

That is how all those who suffer injustice and persecution should proceed; who are victims of the cunning of the wicked and their excessive ambitions; who suffer betrayals and iniquities undeservedly imposed upon them; who always forgive those *who know not what they do*, because their reign of self-satisfaction and ostentation is always fast and chimeric, soon undone, burned by the reality stalking them...

One year had passed since Eneida's marriage to João Pedro, and they were both experiencing the delightful fruit of happiness found in abundance on the tree of true love, understanding and respect that should always exist between partners. Blessed also by religious faith, which enriched them with hopes for the spiritual future, while helping them cope with the normal occurrences of a daily life free of stress and anxiety, they actually thanked God for the suffering they had experienced because, in light of it, they could appreciate the treasures that now embellished their lives.

Shortly after the emotion-packed commemorations of the first anniversary of their marriage, Eneida showed signs of being pregnant, which further enhanced the couple's joys. When she told her mother the news, Evangelina was delighted and could not hold back her tears. The unspeakable jubilation of being a grandmother, of which she had been robbed, had returned. She immediately informed her husband, who was also thrilled, as was Júlio, who was still single, although besieged by beautiful, marriable young women.

The young man had become an inviolable fortress, standing beside his mother and stepfather, whom he loved as his real father. He felt fulfilled in his work, while Spiritist knowledge stretched his existential horizons, filling in any gaps that happened to appear on the inside. He suffered neither conflict nor torment of any kind, which was the result of previous existences, in which he had been celibate for religious reasons, training himself to live an honest, honorable and thus balanced way of life. The only exception was the affective occurrence during his last incarnation, when he had committed the offense with Eneida... Yes, he did want to get married, but he was not in a hurry, which – let us face it – was perfectly normal.

The rush with which young men throw themselves, due to immaturity, into the games of sensuality, irresponsible sex, deviations in moral conduct, and promiscuity only results in disorder, which may turn into deluded flights into drugs, alcohol, tobacco etc. and suicide...

Powerlessness and fear spread within new generations, which, donning the mask of cynicism, meet in tribes, display outrageous behavior, experiment with *cannibalism* and *autophagy* in small degrees, alienating themselves from the social context, while exploiting those who work, fomenting chaos and anarchy. In some cases, these attitudes result from unresolved conflicts and difficulties with adjusting to the social group due to shyness or fears that have terrified them in broken, disorganized, abusive or loveless homes...

Sociologically, many factors work against today's communities, from pressures of all kinds, to the challenges that technology imposes on the market of economic, individual, national and international interests, leading immature individuals to lose control, and confusing many of those that are highly educated, that strive to keep up with the Cyclopean march of progress. Thus not everyone achieves the triumph for which they strive, charging society a high price and making progress difficult, progress that is manifested in electronic machines and appliances, which are not as easy to acquire and handle as the salespersons caught up in mass media say they are.

From the psychological point of view, such factors also encourage the emergence of traumas and existential dramas in today's haphazardly growing communities, with space becoming tighter and nature becoming polluted, adversely affecting everything and everyone. The less able and the more emotionally weak become victims of the dog-eat-dog context and are consumed by grave disturbances.

Júlio, however, had been able to resist such a situation and he equipped himself with values to continue without the constraints that are imposed on so many who opt for wholesome conduct and a well-directed existence.

* * *

The political and administrative situation in South Africa was becoming worse with each passing day. Crime of all sorts was on the loose. Noble voices rose to inveigh against the wave of looting and perversity, of murders and rapes, of increasing vandalism, but the results were far from encouraging.

The threats of revolution were increasing against whites, who were now harassed and openly threatened. Properties suffered depredations; dignified people suffered disrespect; and the shadow of fear was reversing: previously, the ghettos were where those who were discriminated against due to their race and skin color were smothered and excluded; but now their former oppressors – all who had the European epidermis – were the oppressed.

At one of the illuminating meetings held at the Albuquerque's, in a manifestation of psychophony, the spirit mentor urged his friends to make rational arrangements for their own futures and the futures of their families in the troubled country so that they could contribute on behalf of the peace agreement, which was becoming an instrument of cruelty in the hands of yesterday's unfortunates...

At the end of the meeting, the participants discussed the content of the message and began to take the situation much more seriously.

Over the course of the days, Dr. Albuquerque thought it best to explain to his family the plan he had been formulating for some time. He wanted to return to Portugal before things got much worse in the host country. It had always been his dream to return to his beloved homeland. He had cautiously acquired some properties in a Portuguese metropolis, and had sent resources for a long stay devoid of any troubles or worries that might disturb his or his family's future peace.

After listening to him with care and affection, all agreed fully to the need to sell the business, organize their commitments and free themselves from some of the activities with which they were connected, so that they all could travel definitively to their beloved Lusitania, including João Pedro and Eneida, whose pregnancy was progressing smoothly under the blessings of love.

Again, the designs of God were inviting the family to make bold decisions and to foster attitudes requiring courage. Only this time, considering the financial foundation on which they based their resolution, it would be very different from the flight that occurred during the regrettable events in Angola. It is always immensely exciting to return to one's homeland, which seems to have remained so very far away, either by the imposition of a compulsory exile, or one of a more spontaneous nature that circumstances have imposed.

The first step was to put the properties up for sale. A specialized agency was hired, which had no difficulty selling them, in view of the excellence of each one of the residences. Selling the business was more problematic, however, because the apprehension that affected the Albuquerques was also affecting many other families. Some had already moved to the European continent, whereas other families, somewhat apprehensive, were keeping an eye on events in order to determine the course of the future.

Social disorder or politics, and both together, flow normally through the same narrowing funnel, where they become mixed together and, from any point of view, are always synonymous with chaos and tragedy in progress. They start out sneakily; then they settle in and explode in violence, which culminates in total disrespect for established laws, citizenship and human rights, with grave losses for society.

This was exactly the case in a country that was not prepared for the inevitable changes that had begun to increase and which would later become a calamity...

Repressed hatreds, long-held resentments, and the desire for revenge, combined with yearnings for freedom – for which those who used to be excluded are not always prepared due to their lack of experience regarding the duties that result from having rights – became like a bomb under pressure that could explode at any moment. This is because these ungoverned passions, which threatened the leaders themselves, had already been brewing in one way or another, for in the tumult, leaders are incapable of leading the masses, hungry for plunder, for personal revenge, for the delirious thirst for merciless charges.

In cases of this nature, communities always go from an execrable dictatorial regime to one of apparent freedom, during which the most ignoble acts of savagery and impiety are practiced.

It is absolutely necessary that educating the people be given priority in any liberating movement so that they may be prepared for the coming events that will completely alter habits and open doors to new expectations, which must be supported by noble and peaceable methods. These are not times for revenge.

In light of such circumstances, Dr. Albuquerque traveled to Lisbon to visit one of his properties in the city of Z. He planned to move there with his family and wanted to speed up the completion of the comfortable home that had been under construction for some time.

When his relatives living in that city became aware of his decision to bring his family back to the mainland, they were overjoyed.

But when he examined the work being done on the mansion, he saw that those in charge were not following his orders, nor had things gone as smoothly as he had expected. His absence and the lack of personal oversight had led the contractor to overspend the resources that had been sent from Africa, violating the trust that Dr. Albuquerque had placed in him.

Unfortunately, this is a very common characteristic in certain human behaviors. Whenever some individuals receive an important, dignifying job to do, they exploit the situation and think they have the right to act arbitrarily, misusing the resources entrusted to them and using them for their own benefit. Moral failures of this nature have become so common that they have acquired a certain type of citizenship among individuals in whom trust is placed, requiring more caution in commitments and enterprises with others.

Dr. Albuquerque was gifted with a strong intuition. Hence, he had sent furniture, utensils, tableware, bedding, and bath furnishings to Portugal long ago, foreseeing some emergency. He had not wanted his family to go through the bad experiences of the past.

Thus he had also acquired a nice apartment on the outskirts of Lisbon for times that required his or some family member's presence in the capital. The apartment would allow for a continued existence in a climate of harmony, without financial hardship or worries about work.

Consequently, he was able to equip the two homes with what was necessary, after more than a month of personally overseeing the conclusion of the residence he had built in the north of the country, a place of emotional roots from childhood.

Upon returning to South Africa, arrangements were made for Evangelina and Eneida to make the move so they could arrange the residences. Dr. Albuquerque, Júlio and João Pedro would follow later, after having taken care of business matters.

In spite of the prevailing economic situation, as the result of assistance by friends and other influential people, it was not difficult to transfer resources to the homeland, guaranteeing funding for Dr. Albuquerque's future projects.

Two months after the decision to leave the *Dark Continent*, the business was sold at a very good price, considering the prevailing difficulty; and after bidding farewells and wrapping up final details, Dr. Albuquerque, Júlio and João Pedro traveled with their spirits oppressed with nostalgia and with gratitude to those generous and friendly lands, where, at times, they had paid off painful karmic debts, but also where they had had the happy opportunity to build a future full of joy and devoid of economic-financial concerns.

After having moved into the mansion, which stood out in the verdant landscape of the Minho, the first period was highly enjoyable, entailing the comfort of family life, visits to dearly-loved places that time could not erase from memory, and Eneida's happy pregnancy.

Time, however, is a great master that teaches without words. Instead, it uses the experience of personal contact to give valuable lessons that lead to moral and spiritual growth.

The rest of the family in Portugal was still connected with orthodox Catholicism, although they did not study it very seriously – it was more out of habit and ignorance than by principle of rational conviction. They eventually started making negative comments about the behavior of the newcomers, who maintained the weekly habit of Spiritist study in the home. In addition, their non-participation in Sunday church services attracted attention, generating some undue interference by relatives who disapproved. If it had not been for Dr. Albuquerque's tact and diplomacy, it would not have been long before there would have been friction arising from intolerance and disrespect for personal beliefs.

Imposing one's way of thinking on the way one's neighbor is living is an old human habit. Others are to live according to the standards established by arbitrary individuals, who forget that they would never accept their own unreasonable demands if the situation were reversed, thus incurring a very serious error...

With much diplomacy and dignity, the upstanding Spiritist held a reception dinner for all the members of his own and Evangelina's family in his residence, during which he openly exposed his family's convictions. From then on, the subject was closed. None of them were to interfere with the way any of the others behaved religiously.

The guests all nodded in agreement, albeit reluctantly, and promised they would respect the way Dr. Albuquerque's family expressed their communion with God, since they did not intend to pressure anyone to adhere to their faith, a requirement which, in turn, the others would adhere to, to be perfectly fair.

From then on the relationship was a fraternal one, without the possibility of conflicts that might generate unsustainable situations.

* * *

In Magaluf, Manolo's situation was becoming more distressing each day. Sadly, he was still demented, while spiritually he was anathematized by the enemies he had forged through his evil deeds.

His friends gradually became aware of the unfortunate situation, and, as it only happens in terrestrial society, with a few exceptions, they kept their distance in order to save themselves some work or trouble.

Olga was truly possessed of a noble character, and after leaving the securities business and seeking to transfer the company to other interested parties, she continued to do a fine job managing the family assets, advised by an excellent lawyer friend.

In the meantime, Ramiro Alvarez had become aware of the total madness of his colleague-turned-enemy, and devised a plan to get his hands on the diamond set, which he had not gotten out of his ambition-mad mind.

Knowing the métier of the crime, he had no difficulty in attracting two old cronies who had remained in his memory from the earliest days, when he had first arrived in the city, and he devised a sordid plot to get his hands on the gems, which intoxicated him with greed at the prospects of possessing them.

He invited his accomplices for a preliminary meeting near the office, which Olga had not yet sold, and where the diamonds were surely kept in the safe. Ramiro explained to them:

"I know for a fact that the owner will soon divest herself of all her business ventures in order to live on the income, so she will be transferring a number of documents and some jewels from here to some other safe or a bank."

After a brief reflection, he added:

"I remember watching Manolo open the safe. It is in the wall, protected by reinforced concrete girders. In it were various papers and a velvet-lined case wrapped in the same kind of cloth. I'm very interested in that case. It'll be easy; nothing to worry about. We'll go there next Saturday night, after casing the building's surveillance system to find the best way to get in. Then we'll blow the safe."

He paused again and then concluded the ignoble plan:

"One of you will help me immobilize the guard. We'll then take him inside the office and lock him in the bathroom. The other will act as a lookout and watch for anyone who happens to walk in that direction. That won't be very likely; the place is in a somewhat isolated place; plus, it's a weekend, when the area is really deserted...

"Then one of you will help me to set the charge and then tear off the damaged door. We're only going to take the case; that's what's valuable to me. We'll agree on a fee for the job. I'm offering each of you up to a thousand dollars, if everything goes according to plan. That's great pay, after all, for a little job that doesn't have any risk. I'll have a friend prepare the explosives so that we don't get hurt or experience any danger."

Both of the accomplices nodded in utter excitement, and it was settled that they would watch the office during the day and for a few hours at night, especially toward dawn, so that they would reap a good harvest of fruit.

Ramiro had been careful not to say exactly what was in the box he intended to steal, stating that it was gold coins or something like that. He did not want to arouse too much interest on the part of his accomplices – such types always try to extort more, as was the case with he himself.

Thus, the cunning fellow had another acquaintance prepare a small packet of plastic with enough nitroglycerin to blow the safe.

The days passed among anxieties and exacerbation of vile sentiments.

On the appointed day, after midnight, as a haze hung over the city during that mild winter, the three thieves drove in a pickup truck to the objective of their insanity.

They stopped the vehicle some distance away with the headlights off, and the trio waited, watching for any passers-by. There were none. Then, one of them jumped out and went to the building and, approaching the guardhouse where the night watchman was stationed, asked him for information, explaining that his car had broken down and asking him to call a tow-truck.

Unsuspecting and careless, the young man left the guardhouse and was accosted by the assailant, who pointed a revolver at him and told him to open the gate, which he immediately did.

He called the other thugs and immobilized the guard, locking him in the restroom after using his key to open the main door of the office and entering with flashlights.

The cold air seemed to foretell tragedy. Maybe it was the gravity of the crime or anxiety about the robbery.

They placed the charge on the door handle to the safe and covered it with towels to stifle the noise. Then they set the timer and both ran behind the desks for protection. A few seconds later there was an explosion and a deafening noise. The force of the blast blew out the windows, leaving the room steeped in the characteristic smoke and odor.

Immediately afterwards there was dead silence as they waited to see if anyone might have heard the explosion. Since there was no movement outside, the lookout came in and told Ramiro that everything was all right. As the smoke began to clear, they approached the safe with the flashlights. The door was wide-open, and they stood facing the reason for the break-in.

In his anxiety, Ramiro nervously took out the case, stumbled and dropped it. In the fall, the lid shifted and stayed open. The criminals shined their flashlights on the case and were dazzled by the starry glow of the rare gems.

They could not stifle the exclamations that escaped them automatically, and one of them threw himself on the case and eagerly picked it up.

Ramiro could not help himself. He advanced in a rage to take it and the two got in a violent fight with punches and kicks – now in the dark, now in the glow of the flashlights – before Ramiro managed to come up with it. But he did not have time to experience the joy, because the other accomplice stabbed him with a knife, making him tumble, bloodied, to the floor, groaning wildly. The other thief recovered his balance and stabbed Ramiro over and over, leaving him for dead. The two accomplices escaped quickly.

The tragedy was consummated. The cowardly accomplices had reached an unspoken agreement that they deserved the spoils of the crime, and they had joined together to eliminate the instigator, whom they knew to be as evil as they were, or more so.

In the morning, when the relief guard arrived at his post, he was faced with the tragic event. After releasing his exhausted colleague, who was pounding on the bathroom door, the police were called, accompanied by an ambulance for Ramiro. But Ramiro had not survived his wounds, having died hours earlier.

Olga was summoned and discovered that the fabulous necklace and earrings were gone, although various other assets and less costly jewels were intact.

One can understand the extent of her shock, falling into true prostration.

Aided by her lawyer friend, she received appropriate medical care and was taken home. Her mindless husband was not told of the occurrence, since it would finish driving him insane, if he were still actually in possession of some judgement.

Ramiro Alvarez was recognized by the police because he was already known in the department for his drug deals, thefts and robberies. He was buried after the required autopsy, without any great care...

Tragically for him and painfully for Olga, the chapter of precious, ill-fated diamonds had come to an end.

8
THE DAWN OF
A NEW DAY

The news was widely exploited by newspapers, radios and television stations with the usual commotion and the total lack of anything positive.

The comments increased, and Olga received unusual visits from friends, admirers of her possessions, and unscrupulous police officers who set about trying to recover the diamonds by offering a huge reward.

It was a mob anxious to exploit the situation in order to benefit in some way, despite the trouble it caused Olga, which, as usual, was not taken into account.

In this field there is no compassion, no sense of solidarity; on the contrary, these wretches take advantage of the afflictive situations of their neighbor in order to benefit monetarily in some way, even though they come across as being interested in helping or sharing the sorrow. But actually they are bereft of any positive emotion. Of course there are exceptions, but the norm holds true with a surprising number of exploiters.

Nothing more would ever be heard of the diamonds. They were extracted from their respective settings to be sold separately on the continent, as always occurs in in such cases.

The thieves split the unfortunate fruit of their murderous robbery and, at the first opportunity, left for Madrid, where they could sell the stones separately for much less than they were worth. They felt no remorse for the murder; they were delighted at the results of having eliminated their competitor.

All write their own story in the book of destiny. The delusional craving to experience pleasure at any price is always responsible for the rivers of tears and the abysses of suffering that later surprise the foolhardy.

Not infrequently, when certain individuals see others who are mentally handicapped, victimized by serious degenerations, overloaded with unbearable burdens of alienation or incessant misfortunes, they become overwhelmed by questions that flog their mind and heart. Nevertheless, a quick analysis of the desperate practices and the ignoble behaviors that plague society would enable them to understand that the accumulation of so many destructive passions leads to consequences for those who practice them. This is what happens, no doubt. It is only through reincarnation that one can find the proper answers to the superlative anxieties and confusions that assail individuals. Today they reap the sowing of their disrespect toward Life yesterday, in the same way that, changing their attitude and starting to sow resignation, respect, and fruitful work, they prepare their tomorrow, which they will face redeemed and happy.

But it has been asserted that all who are unable to discern and understand their suffering, such as those with anencephaly, autism, and other mental challenges, will never recover, because of their inability to consciously re-educate themselves. However, that is an error, since those who are limited in such ways are repeat offenders who have not taken advantage of the purifying trials they have experienced; rather, they have stubbornly held on to their evil, which now imposes compulsory imprisonment on them for an extended time of spiritual reflection, such that they are incapable of exteriorizing the suffering that hammers at them. They are experiencing pain-filled expiation, bereft of the mental comfort of communicating with the outside world. They are crushed, struggling against their constricting limitation, frequently generating negative reactions in those who take care of them, and who cannot begin to imagine the ignominy that they suffer while imprisoned in the body...

It is imperative that the Law of Love triumph everywhere, commanding wholesome lives, maintaining equilibrium in the cosmos, and preserving the general harmony, for the Law proceeds from the Divinity, who is its source of growth and sustenance.

* * *

Olga felt the anguish of the loss of the fantastic jewels and remained traumatized for a long time, unable to understand how anyone could have known about them. She realized that it had probably been one of Manolo's acquaintances, to whom he had bragged about possessing them. With no alternative, and for the sake of her inner peace, she eventually liberated herself from the memory of the event and the loss of the precious set.

Over the course of the long years that followed, the pretentious Manolo succumbed to complete dementia – the result of a guilty conscience, emotional shocks, and the obstinacy of the obsession. Divorced from his fate, the

Rodríguezes were completely uninterested in him, especially after they learned of the theft of the diamond necklace and earrings. They wondered how he could have raised enough money to buy such a treasure while maintaining a high socioeconomic standard. Resentment and contempt rendered him detestable as a form of punishment for the undiscerning waste of the family's resources.

Individuals forget that, in this world of illusion, all are subject to errors and successes, to happy or unsuccessful experiences. But if they would set their minds on understanding the miseries of others and on forgiving them, they would actually be working for themselves when caught in the webs of their ill-advised behaviors.

* * *

While all of that was transpiring in Magaluf, events in Portugal had taken a completely opposite course.

Those spirits who had come together in well-endured trials of regeneration now enjoyed the blessings of joy, work, and communion with God, having paid their debts before Him.

After they had adapted to life in Portugal, Dr. Albuquerque, Júlio and João Pedro decided to start a company for the construction of apartments and also for the administration of residences and other buildings so that everyone would have the opportunity to work hard for the sake of the future and the preservation of health. After all, work is still the best way to preserve one's health and keep one's life happy, in addition to the fruit it provides monetarily. Even great fortunes have to be maintained and enlarged through right uses that promote progress, avoiding becoming a dead patrimony, while millions of people suffer from unemployment, hunger and misery of all kinds.

They set out to begin the experiment in an area of their own property in the north of the country, next to a famous beach, erecting a set of five buildings with apartments suitable for holidays and summer, and which would be purchased by residents in inland regions or in the capital. The enterprise was begun, requiring engineers, architects, landscapers, and appropriate documentation from the government agencies in charge of the required licenses and from preservers of the environment. It required the redoubled efforts of our *returnees,* as all those who had come back from Africa after the revolution of April 25, 1974 were called...

Under the bountiful winds of happiness, the tireless workers adapted to the new *modus vivendi,* active in their respective duties to bring their plan to fruition.

While they prospered socially and financially, their Spiritist endeavor continued unabated, despite occasional, inelegant references by the priest in the church on Sundays.

In keeping with his character, Dr. Albuquerque preferred to speak directly with the priest about his accusation, rather than relying on comments that came to him second-hand.

Thus, when he felt the time was right, he paid him a visit in the church sacristy and asked if he might have a talk with him. To his surprise, he was kindly accepted.

He began their conversation, explaining:

"Since arriving from Africa, my family and I should have already approached you in order to introduce ourselves and establish fraternal contact. The natural difficulties of our first few months of trying to adapt prevented us from doing so as soon as we should have. I realize that now and I do apologize, asking for your understanding."

"Well, thank you for being so kind, my friend," said the good-natured priest. "In this small town we know everything that happens and we were a bit surprised that you had not looked us up, since that has become the tradition here... Of course I understand what kept you, and I'm happy we finally have the chance to meet."

"Of course," Dr. Albuquerque continued, "you may also be aware of our religious convictions, our weekly home-worship, and our charitable activities, striving to visit the suffering and needy in order to assist them somehow."

"Yes, yes... I know all about that."

"I wish to inform you that I myself was a priest for a while in Africa, but I renounced my vows, according to ecclesiastical requirements, when I decided to marry my wife, with whom I continue to live with dignity. I preferred getting married instead of maintaining a behavior that was incompatible with my character. At the same time, since I am curious about the achievements of science, I became interested in finding out about Spiritism, which appeared in France in the year 1857, with the publication of works by Mr. Allan Kardec. Starting then, I became a sympathizer of the Doctrine, and then, after a time of reflections and study, I became a convinced adherent."

"Strange, such behavior," the priest replied reticently. "I think it would be almost impossible for anyone who has knowledge of Christian theology to adopt the atheistic and demonic behavior that Spiritism is."

"I don't want to get sidetracked from the point of our conversation, and we could discuss that issue sometime in the future. The reason for my visit at present is not to discuss philosophical and religious beliefs, but to inform you, my dear friend, that in my home we carry out activities of this kind and we will continue to do so, in spite of your unfavorable opinion. I would like to remind you that, living in a country that had adopted democratic principles, the inalienable right to freedom of religion is guaranteed, such that we Portuguese can choose the one that best meets our spiritual interests, without the imposition of any dominant belief, as used to be the case."

He paused, and then went on:

"I'm willing to take the matter to court if you continue to defame us with epithets and improper accusations, especially since you do not know us, nor have you studied Spiritism, and are thus in no position to do so. The fraternal attitude that brought me here is to ask you as our kind friend and pastor of many not to forget the words of Jesus when he stated that he had other sheep that were not of that flock, referring of course to the Gentiles, detested by the Jews."

"Well, don't you think it's a bit presumptuous to come here and try to impose on me your way of life in our community?" asked the almost angry priest, who was very pale.

"Not at all. I preferred to introduce myself to you directly in order to clarify any questions rather than remain in the shadows fighting ghosts and making room for unjustifiable considerations on the part of the masses, who are ignorant about existential subtleties. Moreover, I am not imposing my conduct on you, but I am here to tell you how I will conduct myself. I will not allow interference from anyone, because I am a Portuguese citizen who pays taxes, complies with the laws, and respects the Constitution of the country, which today is free from the fetters of the past...

"I would like to add, by way of clarification, that Spiritism is fundamentally based on belief in God, on the immortality of the soul, on its communication, and on reincarnation. Its morality is that of Jesus Christ as found in the Gospel, and which He lived with His apostles, not that which human beings have adapted at their good pleasure. Likewise, the Devil is not part of our convictions, because that mythological figure has life only as long as we hold it in our thought. An evil entity that opposes God is devoid of any legitimacy."

The psychic climate was filled with emotion and apprehension. It was Dr. Albuquerque who rushed to alleviate the situation:

"I invite you to come and meet us at our residence and share a meal with us so that we can have time for an informal conversation, of enlightenment on both sides, which will be fruitful for both of us."

There was cordiality and sincerity in his words. Though displeased, the priest, accustomed to dominating the minds and sentiments of his flock, nodded, somewhat disconcerted, extending his hand in an act of brotherhood, to which the visitor responded.

Thus, a non-aggression pact was established on both sides, even though the newcomers had never been aggressive toward anyone.

The days that followed were rich in expectations, and within the proper term, Eneida experienced the signs of childbirth.

Her obstetrician was called. He was monitoring her, even though he lived in a nearby city. Eneida was taken to the hospital, where her little daughter, named Esperanza – in honor of the one that had been torn from her arms – was born.

The family's joy was beyond description. The girl, who presented herself healthy, without any signs of trauma from gestation, would start a new pilgrimage in the flesh, supported by the fates of love and tenderness in the blessed home that had freed itself from suffering in order to build a better future for its members and, by extension, for all humanity.

On that tepid spring morning in the small town of Z., in Minho, Portugal, Little Esperanza had reincarnated in the nest of happiness that had been unmade by her previous, miserable father...

Life never ceases, and love always triumphs!...

Made in United States
North Haven, CT
03 October 2022